Silkscreen is the world's fav
printing method. It allows you to
print on an almost limitless range
of surfaces, with an almost limitless
range of inks. The visual universe
of the silkscreen is incredibly rich,
and the diversity of effects and
textures makes it the perfect vehicle
to express yourself and hone your
creativity. And as a technique, it
is very easy to pick up, requiring
very little investment to get started.
All of this is what makes screen
printing so varied and absorbing for
enthusiasts and professionals alike.

What can you print?

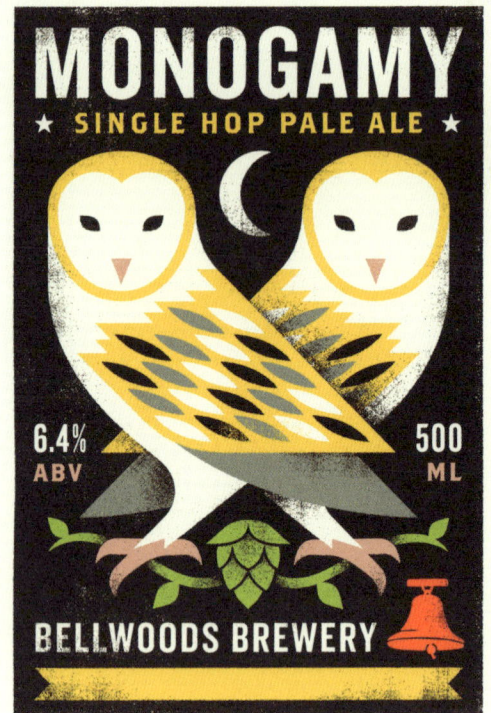

Advert

The warm, handmade visual aura of screen printing makes it well suited for advertising products with similar values, as in the case of this poster for a local micro-brewery, printed by Toronto studio Kid Icarus.

Poster

One of the most common uses of screen printing has always been to produce posters and prints. Here you can see a two-colour poster by legendary French studio Arrache-toi un oeil! for a gig by Jello Biafra in 2013.

Business card

Renowned Greek printer Tind shows how silkscreen can be used to create impactful business cards and other marketing materials. To create this 'fountain' gradient effect, he has printed with two inks alongside each other on the same screen.

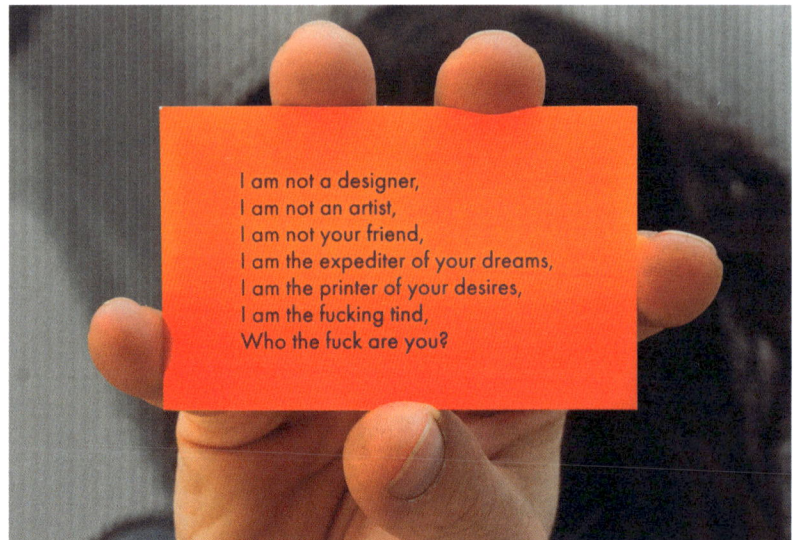

T-shirt

It is incredibly easy to get started screen printing. Many people begin with t-shirts, as you can print cool stuff with quite a basic set-up. This t-shirt printed by Corpoc is a complex design, but only features one colour.

Stationery

Designing and producing stationery is a great way for printers to expand their product line and develop new skills. Seen here are a range of notebooks that Italian studio Legno created for Moleskine.

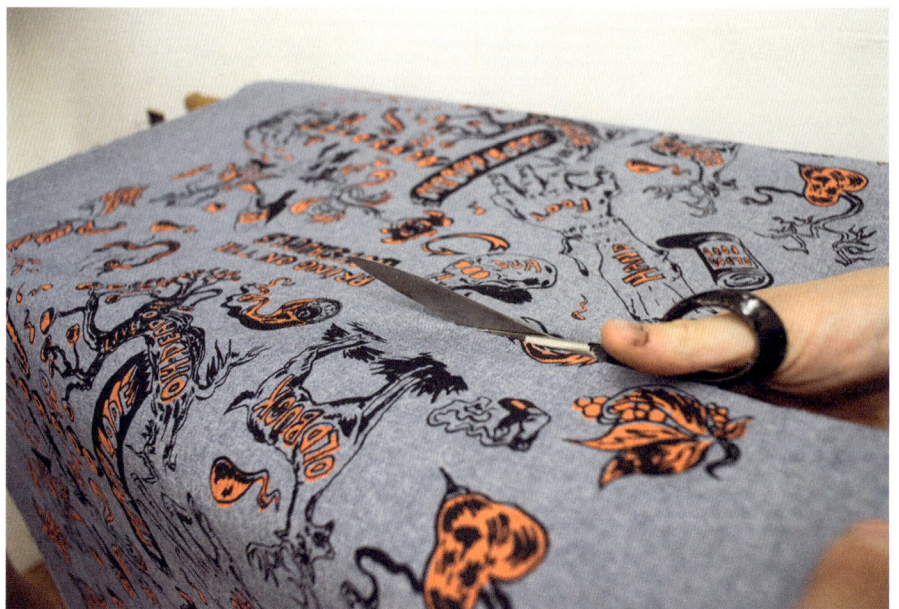

Textile

The textile industry loves silkscreen, in part because it lets you print yard upon yard of fabric. This feature is adapted here by artist Brad Benischek, in collaboration with Italian printmaking collective Print About Me, on his piece 60 YARDS, printed on a long roll of denim.

Comic

Silkscreen is a big favourite among underground publishers, as its low cost and high accessibility help sidestep mainstream printing and distribution models. Le Dernier Cri has been putting out small-run zines and comics (like this one, by Finnish artist Jarno Latva-Nikkola), and other experimental publications since 1993.

Stockings

Stockings are notoriously delicate,
hence hard to print on. French brand Les
Queues de Sardines rose to the challenge
and made a name for itself putting out
collections of hand-printed stockings
in a unique and playful graphic style.

Upholstery

Silkscreen is used widely in furniture and upholstery design, from curtains to cushions to couches. Here you can see a chair with upholstery screen printed by Insley and Nash, a UK workshop.

Scarf

This silk scarf was designed by street artist André (Mr A) for the Circle Gallery in Berlin; you can use screen printing to get a range of colours and subtle tones onto a relatively difficult medium. Photo by Anna Tea

Cassette

Screen printing is the ideal medium for designing packaging for cassettes, such as for these innovative designs and formats from Norwegian studio Drid Machine. As the process is so cheap, you can easily do short runs inexpensively.

Record

This lush 12" was printed by Corpoc for the band OvO, for their Averno/Oblio EP (2014). Cover, sleeve, and the record itself are all printed in gold; the ability to use metallic and effect inks is one of the great advantages of screen printing relative to offset printing.

Leporello

A leporello is a book folded into an accordion-pleat style (also known as a concertina fold). The format is particularly suited to screen printing, as you can print a whole side in one go. This lovely nine-colour leporello — 'Le Jardin d'Hiver', 2013 — was designed by Elisa Talentino and printed at Print About Me in Turin.

Artist book

The versatility of silkscreen makes it perfect for artistic experimentation: there are just so many variables to play with. *Vento* is a book (18 pages, 15 x 19 cm) by Brazilian artist and printer Zansky, head honcho at the Edições de Zaster publishing project; he made 40 copies, each one unique.

Pop-up book

This pop up book is the creation of duo
Mayumi Otero and Raphael Urwiller, who
print and publish as Icinori. The dazzling
complexity of the book is testament to their
creative vision, and to the way silkscreen
lends itself to formal experimentation

Silkscreen Masters

Photograph

One less well known application of silkscreen is to create photographic images. As this image, a printing proof of *Marianne* (2015) by Handsiebdruckerei Kreuzberg shows, you can print images that are as crisp and precise as real photographs, but which exude that intangible richness of screen prints.

Installation

You can use silkscreen to produce projects on a huge scale, as in this installation by Arrache toi un oeil!, produced for the Mo'Fo Festival 2013 in France. According to the creators, its "curves and birds dancing in cosmic clouds" represent "a vision of another planet, or an optical hallucination".

Packaging

This piece by Print About Me is called *Popcorn Explosion* (2014). While popcorn packaging might not be the most cost-effective thing to screen print, this artwork highlights once again the massive flexibility of silkscreen.

Silkscreen Masters

Introduction

Whatever the size of their operation, all screen printers have the same essential needs and face the same essential challenges. While the scope, scale and slickness of their operation may vary, all printers use the same technique. This means that wherever you are in the development of your printing practice, there is plenty in this book of use and interest to you.

Perhaps you have no experience at all, and are simply curious about the technique. Perhaps you have set up a home operation, and are ready to expand into a dedicated space. Perhaps you work in an established design studio that wants to branch out into screen printing. Or perhaps you have some experience of the process and want to start up on your own. In all of these cases and more, this is the book for you.

To put together Silkscreen Masters, we have talked to some of the world's top screen printers, designers, and artists, and tried to distil their accumulated wisdom and experience into a series of steps and tips. On some points, everyone agrees: for example, most people would agree that 'time spent in pre-print is seldom wasted', to adapt an old army adage (in other words, the longer you spend preparing, the better your print will be). On other points, however, there is a whole range of varying approaches. We have tried here to give a space to different perspectives, in order to let you work on the skills you need, while drawing on a database of relevant information and insight.

Silkscreen Masters

Secrets of the World's Top Screen Printers

John Z. Komurki - Luca Bendandi - Dolly Demoratti

MOLESKINE

Table of contents

Gallery FEATURING PRINTS BY

57 serigrafía, Arrache-toi un oeil!, Baker Prints, Chika Ito, Clare Halifax, Corpoc, Crosshair, Damn Fine Print, Daniel Barros, Design & Other, Drid Machine, Gfeller+Hellsgård, Gregory Le Lay, Handsiebdruckerei Kreuzberg, Harvey Lloyd Screens, Harwood King, Heretic, Icinori, Insley and Nash, Jealous Print Studio, Jeffrey Dell, Kate Banazi, Kate Gibb, Kid Icarus, Laurie Hastings, Le Dernier Cri, Legno, Les Queues de Sardines, Lézard Graphique, Lorenz Boegli, Mara Piccione, Margriet Thissen, Medulla, Melanie Yugo, Michelle Miller, Modern Multiples, Mother Drucker, Palefroi, Print About Me, Re:Surgo!, Roland Barth, Serigraffeur, Siebdruck-Corner, Strane Dizioni, Thomas Kühnen, Tind, Tom Kracauer, Viadukt, Zansky.

previous and current spread:
a detail of a print from
Heretic/Spectral Nation

Directory

57 serigrafía
57serigrafia.wordpress.com
Barcelona, Spain

Arrache-toi un oeil!
arrachetoiunoeil.com
Paris, France

Baker Prints
bakerprints.com
Chicago, US

Chika Ito
chikaito.com
s-Hertogenbosch, Netherlands

Clare Halifax
clarehalifax.com
London, UK

Corpoc
corpoc.com
Bergamo, Italy

Crosshair
crosshairchicago.com
Chicago, US

Damn Fine Print
damnfineprint.com
Dublin, Ireland

Daniel Barros
danielbo-art.com
Paris, France

Design & Other
designandother.com.au
Melbourne, Australia

Drid Machine
dridmachine.com
Stavanger, Norway

Gfeller + Hellsgård
gfellerhellsgard.com
Berlin, Germany

Gregory Le Lay
cargocollective.com/lelaygregory
São Miguel, Azores

Handsiebdruckerei Kreuzberg
handsiebdruckerei.de
Berlin, Germany

Harvey Lloyd Screens
harveylloydscreens.co.uk
Wadhurst, UK

Harwood King
harwoodking.eu
Newhaven, UK

Heretic
hereticheretic.co.uk
London, UK

Icinori
icinori.com
Orléans, France

Insley and Nash
insleyandnash.com
London, UK

Jealous Print Studio
jealousprints.com
London, UK

Jeffrey Dell
jeffreydell.com
San Marcos, US

Kate Banazi
katebanazi.com
Sydney, Australia

Kate Gibb
kategibb.co.uk
London, UK

Kid Icarus
kidicarus.ca
Toronto, Canada

Laurie Hastings
lauriehastings.com
London, UK

Le Dernier Cri
lcderniorcri.org
Marseille, France

Legno
sitodilegno.com
Milan, Italy

Les Queues de Sardines
les-queues-de-sardines.com
Bricquebec, France

Lézard Graphique
lezard.fr
Brumath, France

Lorenz Boegli
lorenzboegli.ch
Müntschemier, Switzerland

Mara Piccione
piccione.nl
Groningen, Netherlands

Margriet Thissen
margrietthissen.com
Eindhoven, Netherlands

Medulla
medullamade.com
Modena, Italy

Melanie Yugo
melanieyugo.com
Toronto, Canada

Michelle Miller
michellemillerprint.com
Chicago, US

Modern Multiples
modernmultiples.com
Los Angeles, US

Mother Drucker
motherdrucker.de
Berlin, Germany

Palefroi
palefroi.net
Berlin, Germany

Print About Me
printaboutme.it
Turin, Italy

Re:Surgo!
resurgo-berlin.com
Berlin, Germany

Roland Barth
rolandbarth.com
Berlin, Germany

Serigraffeur
serigraffeur.berta.me
Berlin, Germany

Siebdruck-Corner
siebdruck-corner.com
Berlin, Germany

Strane Dizioni
stranedizioni.org
San Severino Marche, Italy

Thomas Kühnen
thomaskuehnen.tumblr.com
Essen, Germany

Tind
tind.gr
Athens, Greece

Tom Kracauer
tomkracauer.com
Los Angeles, US

Viadukt
viadukt.at
Vienna, Austria

Zansky
zansky.com.br
São Paulo, Brazil

Space

1

The first thing to consider is the space where you are going to screen print. This could be one larger space divided into zones, or several smaller rooms.

For most people, home is where we start from. Building a home studio enables beginners to get up and running with very limited outlay or overheads. The equipment is often rough and ready, but there is no reason why you shouldn't be able to do great screen printing in a scratch-built home studio. This is also the best way to learn on the job and develop your own bespoke workflow.

Sooner or later, though, you will come to a point when you start to think about scaling up. There are a lot of possible reasons – you want to make a living out of screen printing, for example, or set up a community hub. This is when you'll need to increase volume, streamline processes, and guarantee consistency. But whether you have a DIY set-up or are putting together a medium-sized studio, your basic requirements are going to be similar. Your space will be divided into four main areas.

opposite page:
print table at the
Handsiebdruckerei
Kreuzberg studio
in Berlin

Print zone

The print zone is the main area of the studio.

This should be a functional, pleasant space, with enough room and a good source of ventilation. You'll need to pay a lot of mind to feng shui: simply, the more organized you are, the better your printing will be.

This space is also where you will dry your prints and store materials, as well as iron and hang printed fabrics.

Equipment/material

- print table
- screens
- drying rack
- ink
- hinge clamps
- tape
- ruler
- squeegee
- spatula
- spray glue
- apron
- latex gloves
- carousel
- heat gun
- dusk mask
- substrate

Ink-free zone

The ink-free zone is a dedicated space for design work.

Any little improvised area will do, and a desk is often sufficient. However, as this is where you will keep and use your digital and analogue design tools, it needs to be a dedicated space.

This is also a good place to store materials, as well as keep your print archive.

Equipment/material

o computer
o printer
o art supplies
o transparencies
o scotch tape
o scissors
o blank paper
o books
o scissors
o ruler

Dark zone

The dark zone is for coating and drying screens.

This can simply be a cupboard, or a corner of your studio curtained off with thick black fabric. Enemy number one is ultraviolet (UV) light.

Some people coat their screens in a semi-dark environment, but as long as it isn't in direct sunlight, you're okay: just get it into a dark place straight away. A dark or semi-dark effect can be achieved at a pinch with a thick curtain and a red bulb.

Equipment/material

o emulsion
o scoop coater
o exposure unit
o stop watch
o hairdryer or fan
o screen rack
o thick blankets
o glass cleaner
o safe light
o tape
o weights
o blackout

Wash zone

The wash zone is where you clean and reclaim screens.

Here you do anything involving water. The basic elements are a tap and a sink or tub to stand screens in. A pressure hose is highly desirable, but a normal hose will do.

Your wash unit must be a dedicated zone: assume it will never be clean again. Don't forget to waterproof nearby electrical outlets.

Equipment/material

o pressure hose
o stopwatch
o wash unit
o rags
o degreaser
o emulsion remover
o eye protection
o mask
o paper towel
o sponge
o latex gloves
o ghost remover
o reclaimer

I have a smallish studio, just big enough to have my equipment and one assistant working with me. With screen printing, it's possible to do great things with very little experience or equipment.
Lorenz Boegli

Our studio has enough space to experiment, but is human-sized, artisanal, but precise. Our workflow is quite experimental. We know our processes well, so we can try and experiment with new tricks, invent errors, fail more and more, and finally, maybe, find new doors.
Icinori

— In my desire to be efficient,
I am constantly thinking about
the best sequence of steps,
the best movements, to reduce
wasted energy and time.
Jeffrey Dell

— The small size of my working space places limits on the kind of equipment I use, and type of prints I produce. I print using a small exposure unit, small printing rack, and small baseboards with hinges. I create every piece by hand; there are no large machines with squeegee arms, or carousels. Every piece of furniture in the space serves a dual purpose, or is on wheels. The washout area is towards the back and there is enough table space that printing is separated from preparing artwork, exposing screens, and paper cutting. I have come up with some very creative solutions for storage and equipment. I am constantly reorganizing the space in order to print as efficiently as possible.
Melanie Yugo

Material and equipment

2

Your spaces are set up. Now you're going to kit them out with all the equipment and materials you need to print.

As with spaces, all screen printers use the same range of basic equipment: the screen itself, the scoop, the emulsion, and the squeegee, as well as a host of other items, from useful bits of wood to latex gloves. Where DIY and more established print studios differ is in the machines they use. It is possible to screen print using a table and two pairs of hands, but if you want to expand your operation, investing in a print table is a no-brainer.

When it comes to materials, there are a lot of things to bear in mind, on top of the usual considerations of price and quality. Precision is fundamental. You should not, for example, combine inks from different manufacturers, as they may behave differently.

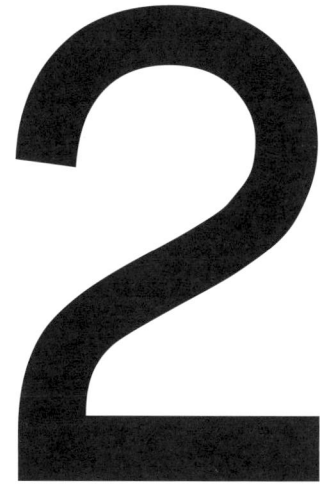

opposite page:
a spatula, scales and
accreted ink at Harvey
Lloyd Screens, a UK studio
in founded in 1976

Screen

The screen is one of the most important elements of the screen printing process. It is a composite of a frame and a mesh.

Wood or aluminium
Frames can be made of either. Wood is cheaper, but heavier and less durable. Aluminium costs more and lasts forever.

Pre-prepared or DIY
You can restretch a mesh yourself with a wood frame, but an aluminium one calls for a mechanical stretcher.

Mesh
Today, rather than silk, mesh is made of polyester threads.

There are two species of mesh: white and yellow.

White mesh takes less time to expose, but isn't so good at handling detail. Yellow mesh is better for detail, but costs slightly more.

Then there are many different sub-varieties of mesh, used for different applications. We distinguish them by their mesh counts, which are usually measured in threads per inch (in the US), or per centimetre (everywhere else). A mesh with a 90 tpcm mesh count has 90 threads running horizontally and ninety threads running vertically across every square centimetre of the screen.

The ink passes between the tiny holes created by the overlaid threads. Logically, if you increase the tpcm, you will have more threads for every centimetre. These threads will be finer, and the holes they create will be smaller, allowing for greater detail.

Think of these holes as corresponding to pixels: higher mesh count = more and finer threads = more pixels = more detail.

opposite page:
Print About Me
—
Massimo Turato
Mole, 2016
solar-exposed screen print; part of the maivisti.it festival, a project by Arteco

below:
different meshes serve different purposes: the more fibres there are, the more detail you can print

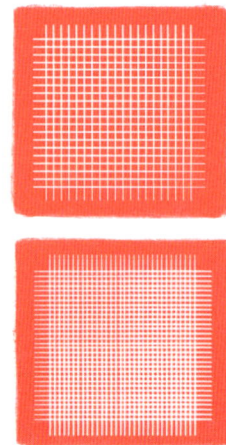

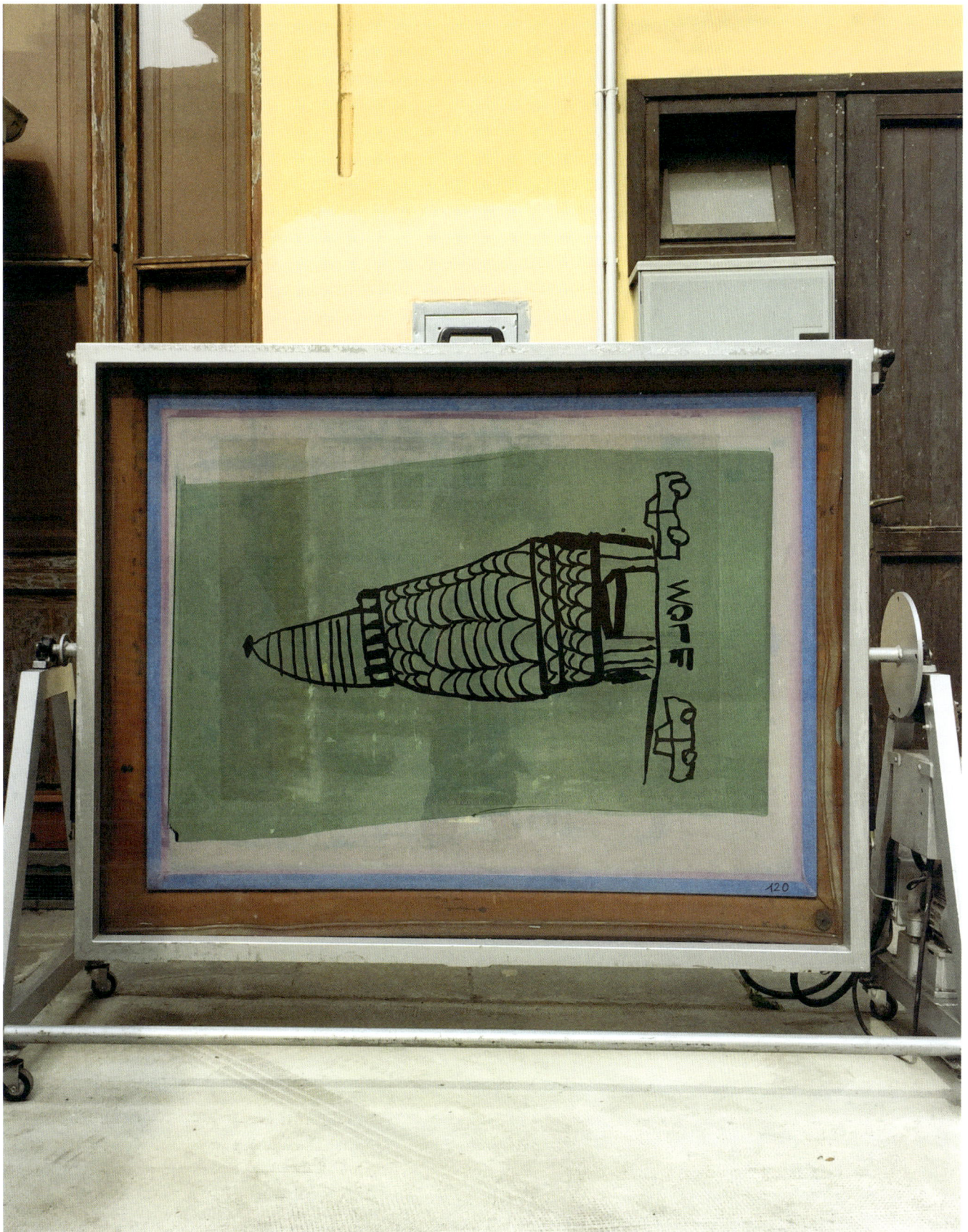

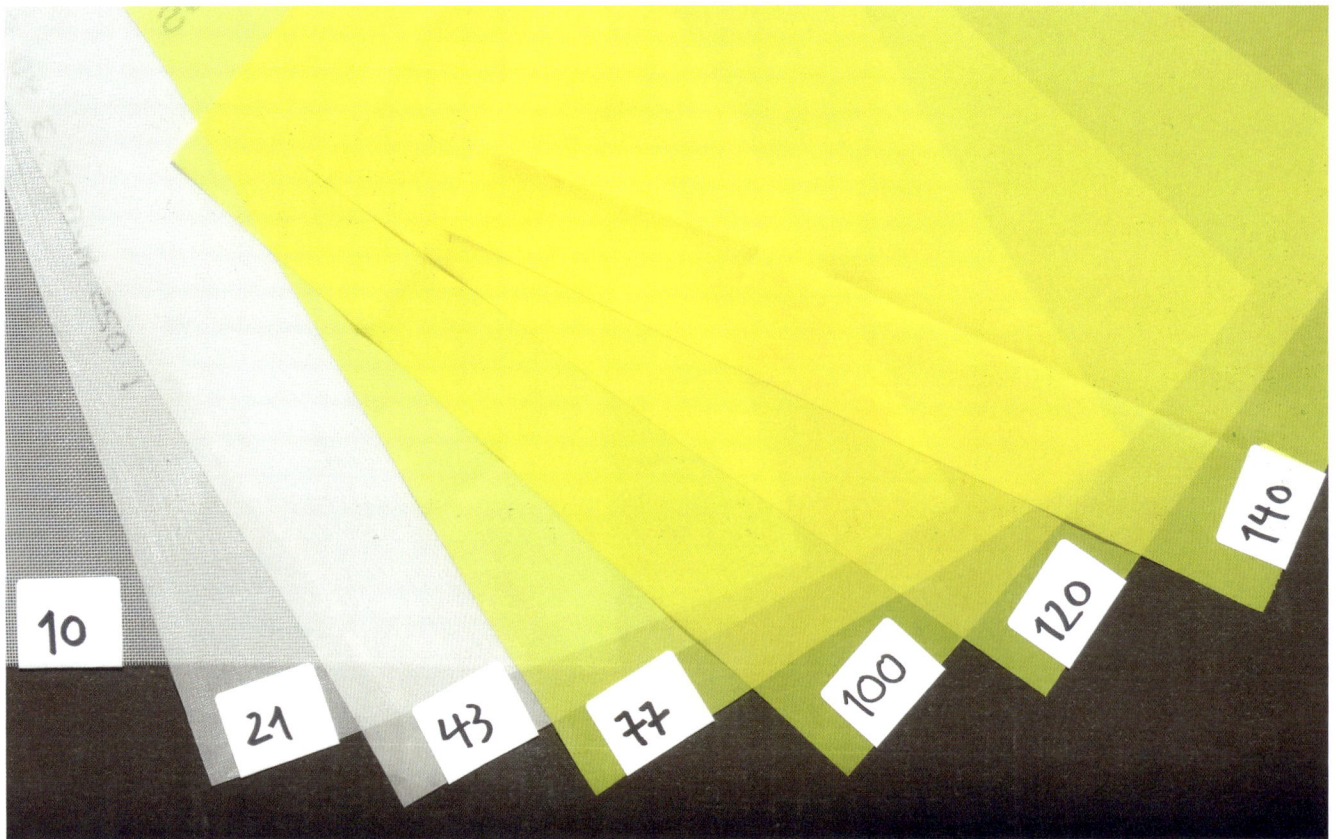

I find most screen printers that are new to the process try and use every inch of the screen. For multicoloured prints, only use the middle of the screen. A stencil around the edges usually warps the image.
Kid Icarus

above:
a display of different varieties of mesh at Handsiebdruckerei Kreuzberg in Berlin

Mesh count finder

Threads/ inch	Threads/ cm		Suggested use	
30	12		For inks with particles that can't pass through finer meshes, such as glitter or shimmer inks.	
60	24		For athletic printing, opaque ink deposits, puff ink, and shimmer ink.	
85	34		For heavy coverage on dark shirts, solid underbase prints, puff, metallic, and shimmer inks, as well as transfer printing.	
125	49		For general printing on dark shirts, underbase prints with detail, prints on dark nylon jackets, and silver shimmer ink.	**Textile printing standard**
190	77		For heavy varnish on paper, details on textile, multicolour printing on light shirts and light-coloured nylon jackets.	**Middle ground to print on both textile and paper**
230	90		For detailed multicolour printing on light shirts, light nylon jackets, and overprinting on dark shirts. Good for photographic halftones and to avoid moiré effect.	**Paper printing standard**
305	120		For process colour on light shirts, overprinting on dark shirts, textured images, and true grain transparency. Works best with short exposure time.	

Squeegee

This is the tool that pushes ink through the screen. Any hard edge will do, but a polyurethane squeegee is best. The squeegee you use should extend a couple of centimetres off both edges of your design, while still fitting inside the screen.

There are different levels of hardness. A harder blade deposits less ink, so the image is crisper. By the same token, coarse meshes work best with a softer blade, while fine mesh requires a harder one.

Squeegees get harder with age. Store them blade-up at room temperature. Remember that the slightest imperfection in the blade can rip a screen.

Film positive

The film positive must be a transparent sheet with a design printed or drawn on it in black. You use this to transfer your design onto the screen, using a techinque similar to the photographic process.

There are many options for your transparent sheet (or transparency), from homemade oiled paper, to acetate and vellum, photocopies on clear foil, or nifty true grain paper.

If you want to print two or more colours, you will need to make a film positive corresponding to each different colour.

Emulsion

This is a light-sensitive chemical mix with which you coat your screen. Your emulsion needs are defined by your printing needs: for example, the light source you use for exposure (some emulsions take longer than others) or the ink (water-based ink calls for water-resistant emulsion).

Emulsions also vary in terms of quality and shelf life (count on an average of four months when refrigerated). You need to mix most emulsions with sensitizer before you can use them; avoid pre-mixed ones.

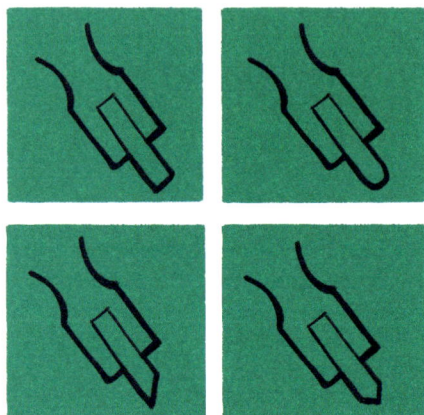

left:
the square edge is the most common and versatile, while the rounded edge is for dealing with a lot of ink; the single-sided bevel is designed for precision, and the double-sided bevel suits uneven surfaces

Scoop coater

Used to apply a thin, uniform layer of photo emulsion to the screen. Can be improvised, but a decent aluminium scoop coater is a worthwhile investment. Its basic function is to combine a reservoir of emulsion with a dull flat edge.

Hinge clamps

To print, all you need is a flat surface and some of these to hold your screen in place. They can be bought from a supplier or art shop. A cheaper alternative is a friend with two hands. A more expensive alternative is a print table.

Exposure unit

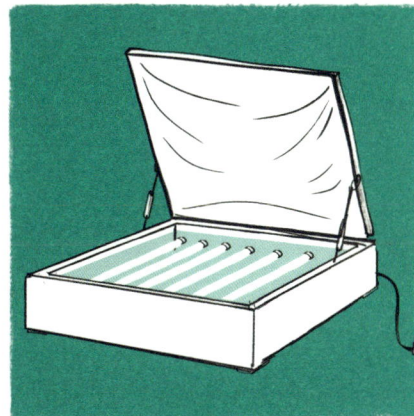

Screen exposure time depends heavily on your exposure unit. The more powerful it is, the quicker you will be able to expose your screens, and the more detail you will get out of them.

Spatula

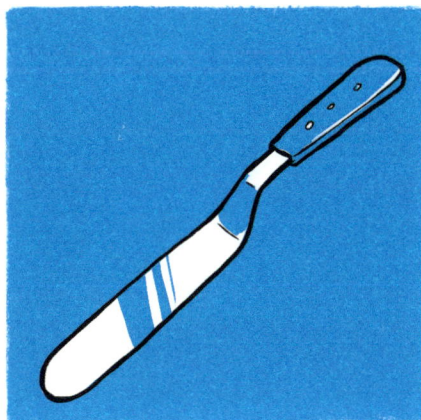

The spatula is for mixing ink and scooping up emulsion, as well as a range of other tasks. You can cut corners here, but it is worth having a set of dedicated spatulas.

Heat gun

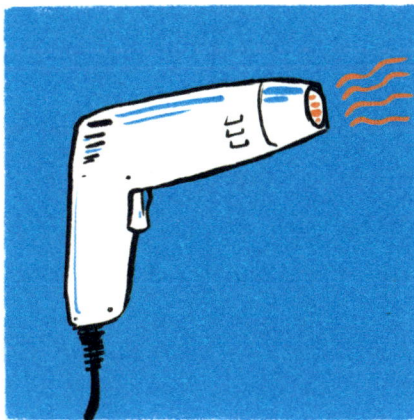

The heat gun is used to fix designs on textiles, so they don't run in the wash. Some inks can only dry when they are heat-treated.

Chemicals

Drying rack

Print table

Degreaser. Grease stains are often invisible, but will build up where the mesh has been handled. Soap or detergent works just as well (as long as it doesn't contain lanolin, an oil).

Reclaimer. A chemical to remove the emulsion from your screen. Some people make do with a bleach/water mix, but it's horrible stuff, and in any case reclaimer is very cheap.

Retarder/reducer. Mixed with the ink so that it stays wet longer when it's on the screen. This is most commonly used with screens that have a higher mesh count.

Fixative. Only used with textile ink. Stops the designs coming off in the washing machine. Mix it with ink at between a 1% and 3% ratio.

Screen filler. More for finer meshes, this touches up small imperfections in the blocking.

Anti-ghost. An extremely strong chemical used when reclaiming to purge any stains on your screens, leaving them spotless. Careful, it burns through the mesh if left on too long.

One solution to drying is to peg prints to a line. This is already better than laying them on your bedroom floor, but there's still a lot of potential for something to go wrong. A drying rack makes life much easier.

Carousel

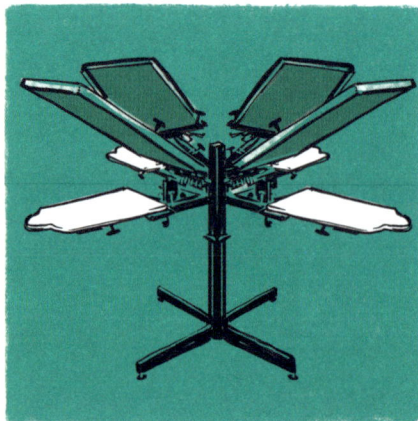

This is an invaluable piece of equipment if you are printing on fabrics: print ten t-shirts in only a little more time than it takes to print one. As with the print table, this will also enable you to concentrate on more than the basic mechanics of printing.

One of a printer's first major investments, it makes the printing process easier, smoother, and more precise. The print arm applies even pressure, while the vacuum holds the paper in place.

Pressure hose

While you can make do with a normal hose, a pressure hose is far and away the best solution to your water needs, helping you clean screens more quickly and effectively.

08:30 SNOOZE
08:37 SNOOZE
08:44 SNOOZE
08:51 SNOOZE
08:58 SNOOZE
09:05 SNOOZE

The skill of a craftsman is in overcoming his tools. For silkscreen, this means when the mesh is invisible in print results, when the register is perfect, and the fineness of detail greater than is usually expected from screen prints.
Lorenz Boegli

below:
Tind brandishing his
ink-laden squeegee; the
mixture of inks is used to
create a fountain effect

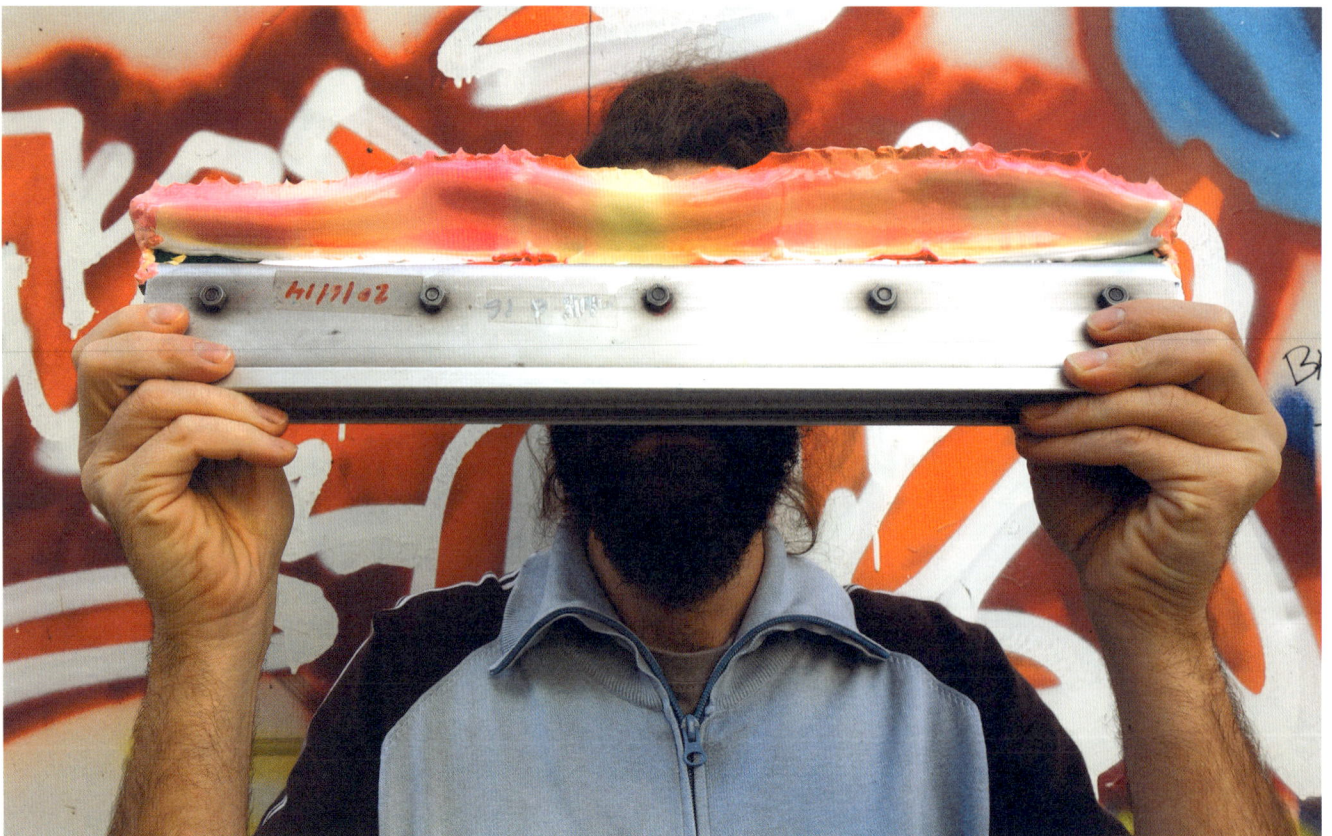

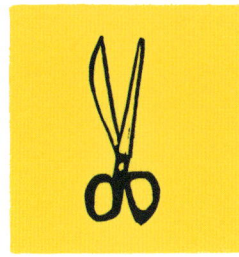

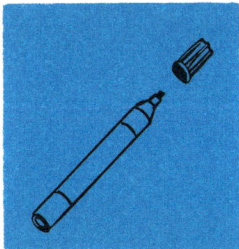

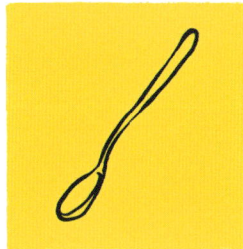

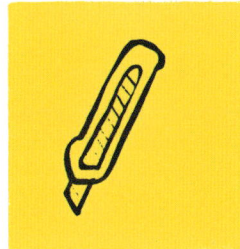

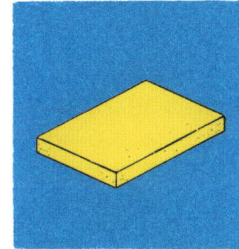

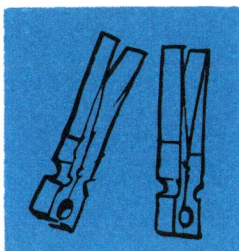

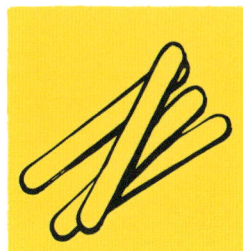

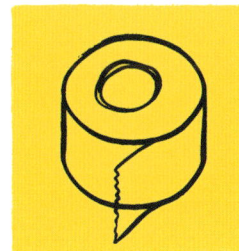

sponge	t-square	coins	scissors	red bulb
ruler	dust mask	brush	hanger	clips
marker	spoon	spray glue	scrub sponge	stopwatch
cloth	weights	utility knife	glass	latex gloves
pegs	wood spatula	container	kitchen paper	clear tape

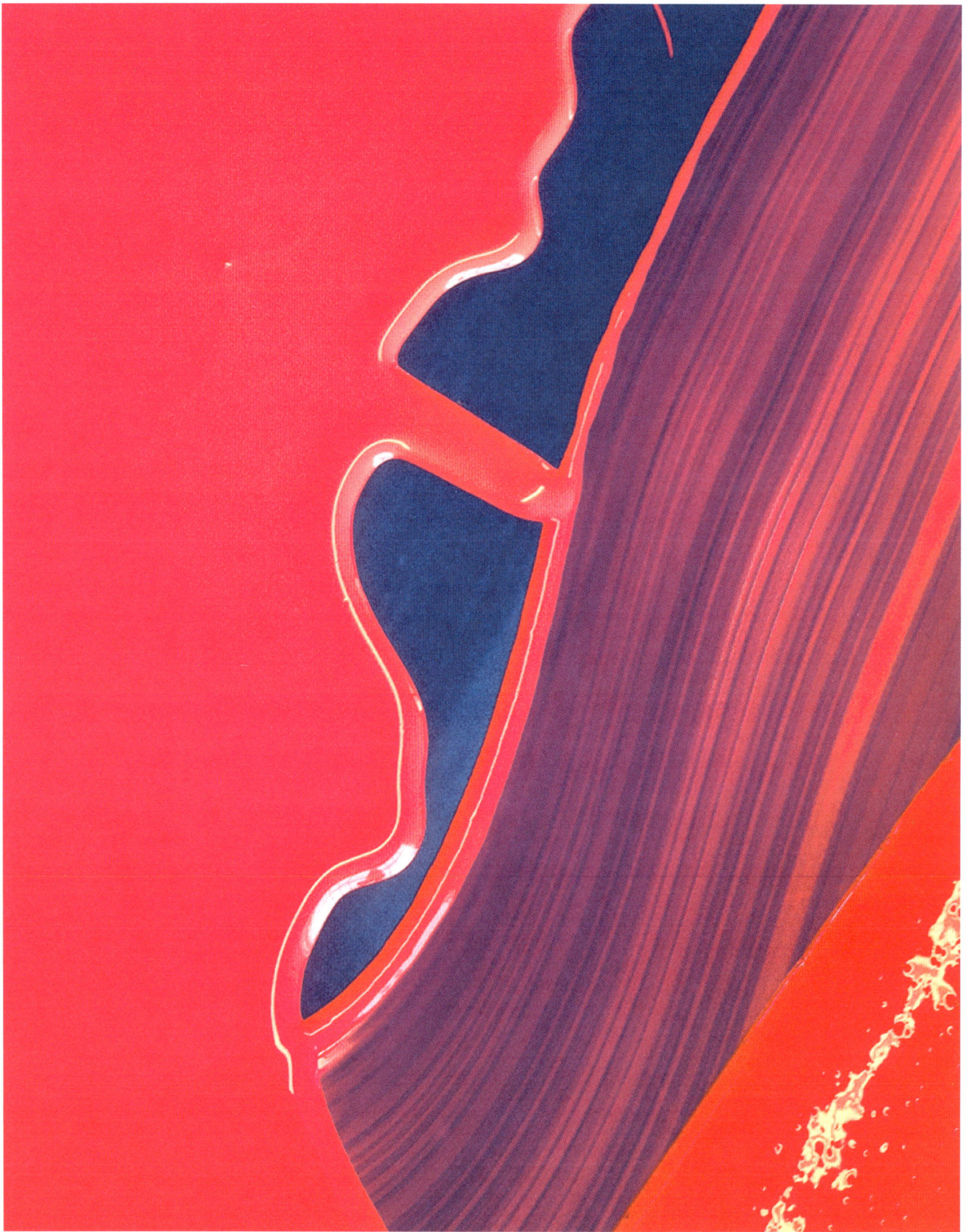

Silkscreen Masters

Ink

Inks are a mixture of pigment and binder. The binder or base is what enables the pigment to stick to the surface it is printed on. There are different types and opacities of binder, from transparent to pearl white.

Pigment comes as either liquid or powder. It is what gives the ink its colour.

If you are just starting out, it is best to use premixed inks. You can buy pigment and binder and mix your own inks (pigment and binder should always come from the same manufacturer).

Binder falls into two main categories: water-based and solvent-based. We also use these terms to talk about the inks themselves.

It is worth noting that, while screen-print veterans may have a kneejerk objection to water-based inks, in the last ten years the technology has come on in leaps and bounds. These days you can do almost everything you might want to do with water-based inks. What's more, solvent-based inks are bad for you and for the environment.

There is a range of specialist inks:

o **neon inks**

o **metallic** or **shimmer inks**

o **glow in the dark inks**

o **photochromic inks,** that change colour in sunlight

o **thermochromic inks**, that change colour when heated

o **prisma inks**, that replicate RGB effects

o **glitter inks**, with suspended glittery particles

o **discharge inks**, which have an effect on textiles similar to bleaching

o **puff inks**, that when heated swell up, creating a 3D texture

o **suede ink**, a puff ink that gives a smooth finish

o **reflective inks**, used for things like hi-vis

o **nylobond**, for printing on water-proof textiles

...alongside various others – it is well worth asking your supplier to show you round their store room.

A range of fluorescent inks are good to keep on the shelf and can be added into other colours to add some strength. **Harvey Lloyd Screens**

opposite page:
ink at Harvey Lloyd Screens, with a thrilling close-up of a neon rainbow effect

Substrate

The substrate is the name for the surface you print onto. Paper and textile are the most common substrates, but in principle you can print on practically any surface, as long as the ink can dry on it. Screen printing is also used at an industrial level in the manufacture of everything from circuit boards to pinball machines.

Paper

Most paper is made either from recycled fabrics or organic pulp. It comes in many varieties and brands, often sold under different names in different countries.

Certain types of paper are better suited to certain processes. Smoother paper will give you the best results when printing halftones, for example.

Take into account the thickness of the paper. Thicker paper absorbs more ink and is more stable, while thinner paper folds more easily (important if you plan to print a fanzine, for instance).

Textile

You can print on virtually any kind of textile, although most people stick to t-shirts and tote bags.

The trick is in choosing the right combination of ink and substrate. A heavy plastisol design on a skimpy cotton t-shirt will look wrong, no matter how good the print itself is.

A print that works well on paper will not necessarily work so well on fabric. Thick, dense patches of ink will feel uncomfortable on clothing.

opposite page: different types of paper have different characteristics; a neatly classified selection at Handsiebdruckerei Kreuzberg

Hersteller Gangolf Ulbricht Qualität Oberfläche
Format Laufrichtung Farbe g/m² Material
Hand
Format Laufrichtung Farbe g/m² Material
Hand Flachs
Format Laufrichtung Farbe g/m² Material
Hand
Hersteller Gangolf Ulbricht
Format Laufrichtung
Hand
Hersteller Gangolf Ulbricht Qualität 137 Oberfläche
Format 50x78 Laufrichtung Hand Farbe g/m² Material
Hersteller Gangolf Ulbricht Qualität Oberfläche
Format Laufrichtung Farbe g/m² Material
Hand
Hersteller Gangolf Ulbricht Qualität Oberfläche
Format Laufrichtung Farbe g/m² Material
Hand
Hersteller Gangolf Ulbricht Qualität Oberfläche
Format Laufrichtung Farbe g/m² Material
Hand

Under artificial light, or even on a cloudy day, a printed colour could seem dark red or smooth yellow, and the day after it's an explosive orange. Fluorescent inks in particular need to be chosen in sunlight. Having bad light is like being colour blind.
Icinori

Textile is easier than paper to start out with, because the results are immediate: you don't have to make fifty prints of one colour, only to find out that the second colour won't align.
Matze from Siebdruck-Corner

Mix your inks three times longer than you think you should.
Michelle Miller

Never print on paper that is straight off the pallet – always leave it in the rack overnight, so it can adjust to the atmospheric conditions of your printing space. Consistent humidity is important – always keep your windows closed (industrial printers even dust the air with water sprinklers). Between 40 and 70 humidity is optimum.
Hansiebdruckerei Kreuzberg

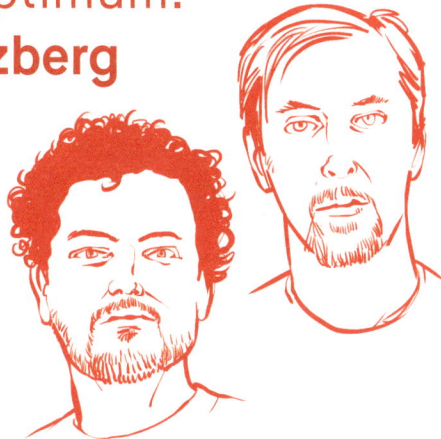

In Australia, using water-based inks can be challenging: battling the heat and humidity is draining physically and mentally, and can affect the print process.
Kate Banazi

Preparing the film positive

3

All your tools and materials are neatly arrayed and you have an idea of what you want to screen print. Now you need to get that idea out of your head and onto the screen. This you do by creating a film positive, either with a computer program or by hand, and transferring your image to the screen.

Remember that, regardless of the colour(s) of the eventual print, the design on the film positive must always be in black (or grayscale). This is because the process you use to create the screen is based on a contact printing method, as we will see in the next chapter.

As with many aspects of screen printing, there is more than one way to skin a cat when it comes to design. The trick here is to experiment as widely and freely as possible. Many printers will tell you that it can be counterproductive to come to the process with a fully formed design; it is often more rewarding to let your design evolve in collaboration with the medium.

opposite page:
a hand-pulled screen
print on Perspex by
innovative Sydney-
based artist and
printmaker Kate Banazi

Analogue design

There are many different approaches to designing for silkscreen without using a computer.

One option is to work directly on the transparency with markers or inks, or by sticking opaque shapes on it. Another possibility is to create your design on paper and then trace it onto the transparency. The crucial thing is that the black is dense, or else the quality on the screen will be low.

Drawing or painting

You can sketch a design in pencil and go over it in marker to get the thick black you need. A very detailed drawing will need a very fine mesh.

Scratching, smudging, and blurring directly on the transparency will give it a touch that you cannot replicate on a computer.

One colour transparency

Create your film positive, either by tracing or drawing onto the transparency. This done, you are good to go for single-colour printing.

Multicolour transparency

If your goal is to make a multicolour print, you have to split the design into its different component colours, then make a separate film positive for each one.

Digital design

Another way to prepare your design is to use image editing software. Options include Adobe Photoshop or Illustrator, or open-source alternatives like Gimp or Inkscape.

You either create your design directly inside the program, or input a prepared image.

While it is relatively easy to print flat colours, some extra steps are needed to get gradients. We explain this process – called halftoning – in detail over the following pages.

Design

Prepare your design. With both raster and vectorial illustrations, if the colours are flat (no fadings or gradients), just set the intended size for the print and prepare the file for printing.

Print

Print using a normal ink-jet printer with a matt black ink cartridge. Change the print settings or use RIP software so it prints with a heavier deposit of ink.

Align

If you are printing more than one colour, after applying trapping (see next page), print each separate colour onto a different transparency. Lay your film positives on top of each other and make sure they line up.

Trapping

Trapping is a technique employed at the design stage to reduce imprecisions in printing and help guarantee good registration. It is used when different colours in a multicoloured print touch each other (or 'butt'). The idea is that there be no white paper showing between them. Make certain areas of colour slightly wider than they need to be, so that if other colours are slightly misregistered, they won't leave even a whisker of white. This means that the bottom colour (the one you print first) 'bleeds' under the top colour. You can achieve this both with software and by hand.

1.   2.   3.   4.

Raster image (Photoshop)

Select your area. From the 'Select' menu: > Modify > Expand selection. Add some pixels and fill them with the same colour. Alternatively, contract the top layer.

Vector image (Illustrator)

Select your area and add an outline stroke.

1. your image

2. print with no trapping

3. print with trapping, perfectly centered

4. print with trapping; registration slightly off, but no white showing

DIY film positive

Pour oil

This is the cheapest (and messiest) way to create a film positive.

First, apply oil to a normal sheet of paper with your design printed on it.

Spread oil

Spread the oil evenly and thinly with a sponge.

Transparent

The oil is absorbed, rendering the paper transparent and ready to use as a film positive.

Printing halftones

A gradient is a patch of colour which fades in intensity from darker to lighter. To achieve a fading effect in screen printing, we need to use a technique called halftoning.

A halftone is a pattern of tiny shapes which, seen together, create an effect of variation in intensity. By using different layers of halftones, we can create an effect which is similar to a photograph.

Black and white

Open a black and white image or convert to greyscale a colour one.

Convert to greyscale

In the 'Image' menu, check the mode setting is greyscale. Play around with contrast and brightness. Bear in mind that the printing process will darken it slightly. When you are ready, set the final size of the print.

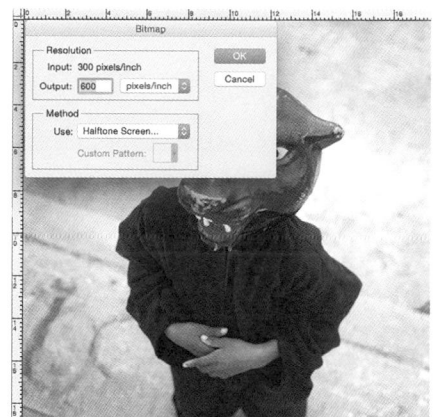

Grayscale to bitmap

From the 'Image' menu select:
> Mode > Bitmap.

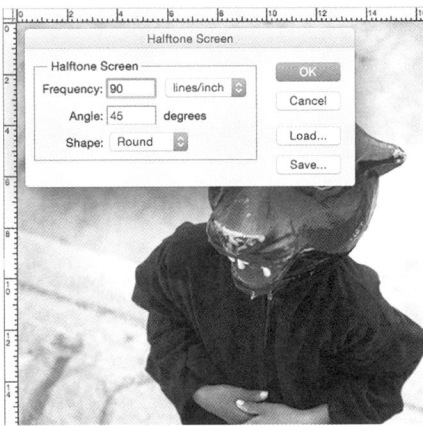

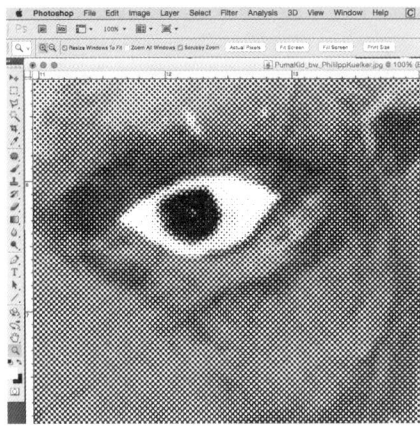

Halftoning

Choose a frequency. The higher the frequency, the finer the pattern will be. Keep in mind the ink and substrate you are using. The angle of the pattern has to be different from that of the threads in your mesh, in order to avoid the moiré effect (see following pages).

Halftone pattern

Print a sample of your image on a normal piece of paper (take care not to let the printer scale it). This is necessary to get a sense of how the final result will be: don't trust the computer screen.

left:
Puma Kid by Philipp Külker, a black and white photo prior to halftoning

above:
a detail amplified at a 1:1 scale after halftoning

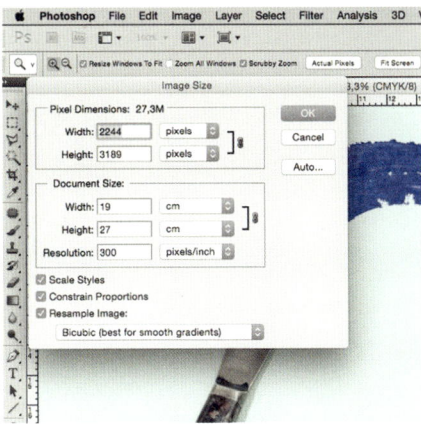

Colour halftoning

Open the file and set the size of the image.

CMYK

From the 'Image' menu select:
> Mode > CMYK colour.

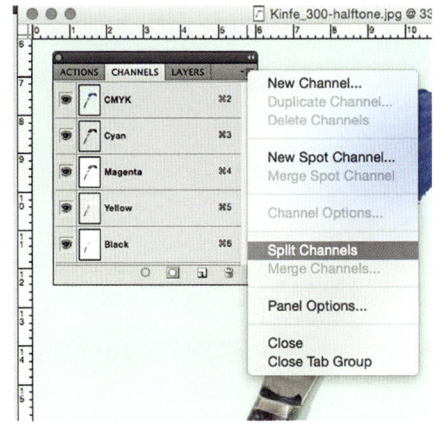

Splitting channels

Now save a copy of your original file. The next step will change it irrevocably.

In the 'Window' menu select: > Channel. From the menu in the upper right select: > Split channels.

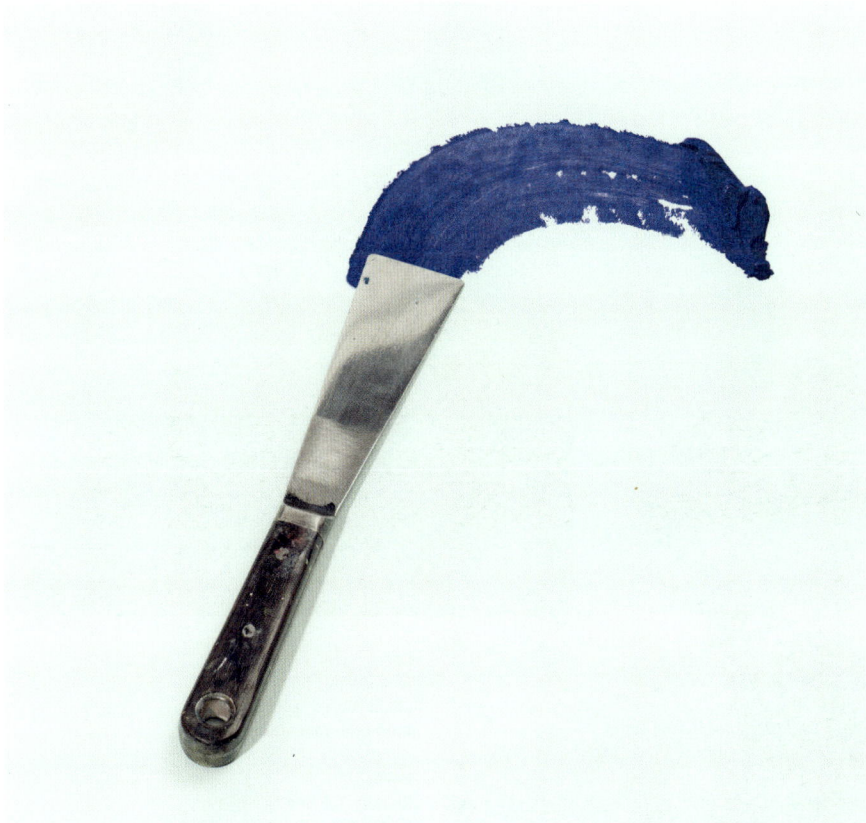

left:
spatula and ink
smear taken at the
Mother Drucker print
studio in Berlin

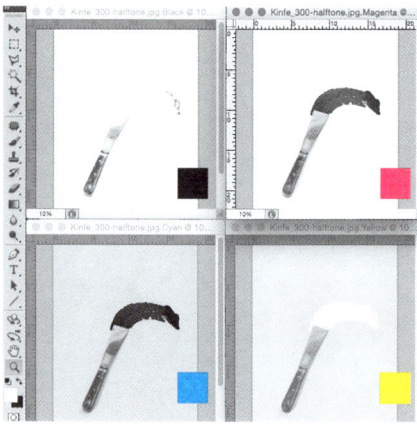

Separate colours

Now the software will create a separate file for each of the cyan, magenta, yellow, and black channels, each one in greyscale.

Halftoning on different angles

Now for each of the files, from the 'Image' menu select: > Mode > Bitmap > Halftone screen.

To avoid moiré, keep the same frequency, but change the angles, increasing them 30° each time: black 45° / magenta 75° / cyan 15° / yellow 0°.

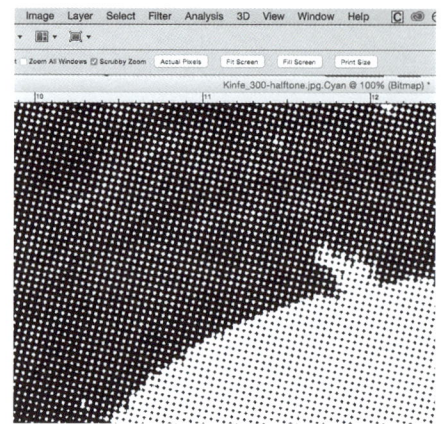

Result

Each channel will be broken down into a halftone pattern.

The colours will be printed on top of each other, creating an effect that from a distance approximates the full colour spectrum.

— The key to a good print job is to separate the colour layers at the beginning on the computer, adding the underpinning correctly. If you spend time at this stage your end result will be better.
Harvey Lloyd Screens

opposite page:
a detail of *Inward infinity*, a four-colour print from Heretic/ Spectral Nation (2015)

Moiré effect

The moiré effect is the term we use to denote a clash of patterns. It can occur when the pattern of the mesh fabric clashes with the pattern of the halftone line count. It can also occur when two halftone patterns from two different screens are badly aligned (see images on the right).

The most common remedy is to make sure the angles of your halftone patterns are consistently different, at intervals of at least 30°.

below:
The Constitution of Moiré, a print by Tind that uses the moiré effect to an unexpected creative end

opposite page:
Error Is Superior To Art, another artwork by Tind that explores the use of moiré aesthetic

BERLIN GmbH PET 1500.100/255-40 GELB-27-03-2017-KUNDE:HANDSIEBDRUCKEREI KREUZBERG

Preparing the screen

4

So your design has been transferred to the film positive, which is now ready to use. The next step is to get your design from the film positive to the screen itself. To do this, you first need to coat the screen in photo emulsion, and then, with the same basic process they use to develop photographs, you will 'expose' or 'burn' it with the film positive.

There are a lot of variables here, largely related to your set up. The technique and equipment you use to burn the screen will define how you approach the task. Secondary factors, such as how much natural light enters your studio, must also have an impact on your workflow.

But as ever the essence of the operation is the same for everyone. Get a good grip on the basics and lay the groundwork for deeper investigation and refinement of your tactics.

opposite page:
a huge screen at Handsiebdruckerei Kreuzberg, used for printing a record sleeve for Moderat

Coating the screen

The goal here is to apply a thin, even coat of emulsion to the screen. Some people prefer to coat screens in a semi-dark environment, but as long as it is not in direct sunlight, you can leave a screen out for a few minutes before the emulsion begins to harden.

Bear in mind that some mesh counts need more emulsion than others. A strong default option is to coat both sides of the screen. Finish on the squeegee side, so that most of the emulsion ends up on the side exposed to the lights.

Checklist

o emulsion
o sensitizer
o spatula
o scoop coater
o screen

Mix emulsion

Mix up some emulsion. Leave an hour for any bubbles to disappear.

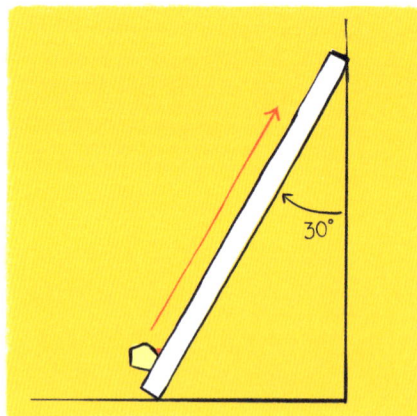

Prop and secure

Lean screen, print side up, against the wall at around a 30° angle – this will help you to coat the screen evenly, and reduce drips. Find a solution, such as a nail banged into the wall, to stop it slipping.

Emulsion into coater

Fill your coater with emulsion.

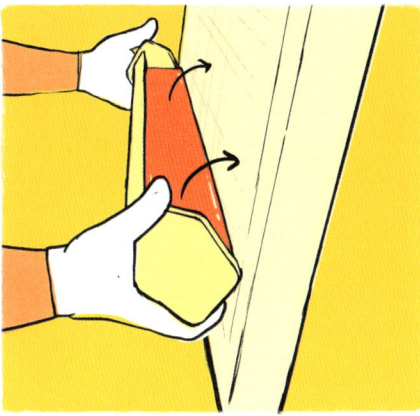

Coater to frame

Place the coater at the bottom of the frame, with the edge touching the mesh. Tilt it forwards.

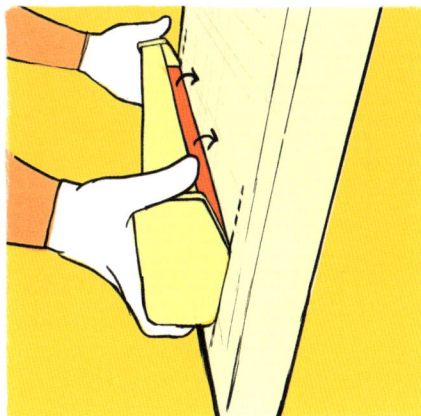

Start to slide

With the coater, and hence the emulsion, now in contact with the frame, start to slide it upwards.

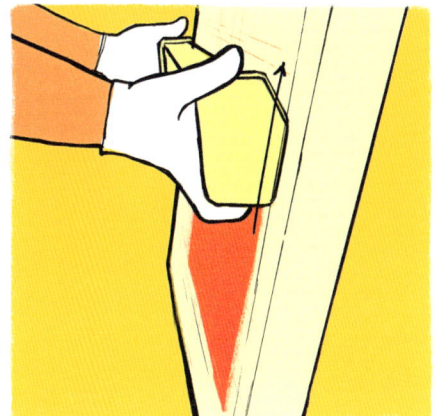

Slide up

Slide it slowly, firmly, and evenly upwards, making sure the edge is always in contact with the screen. As you approach the top of the frame, slow down.

Tilt

When you can drag it upwards no further, stop, and tilt the coater towards you so excess emulsion collects. Then pull it away neatly, at the same time turning it towards you slightly, so the emulsion doesn't run over or drip.

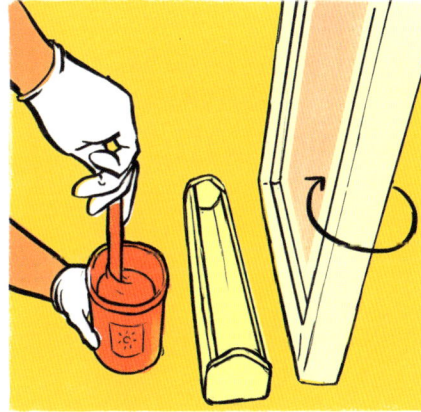

Flip

Turn the screen round and repeat the process. If your layer of emulsion isn't thin enough, scrape off excess with a clean coater. Too much emulsion makes exposure time unpredictable.

Scoop

Both sides coated, scoop as much emulsion as possible from the coater back into the container. Clean the coater well with water.

Leave to dry

Lay the screen horizontally in your dark zone to dry. Alternatively, stand it upright in a warm space, but it has to dry before the emulsion slithers downwards. You can use a hairdryer, heater or dehumidifier to speed things up.

Let dry

The time it takes to dry varies according to factors such as environmental temperature or mesh count.

Patience

Remember that even if the screen is dry to the touch, this does not necessarily mean that all the fibres have dried.

Beginning from prepping the films, a good printer will spot potential problems even before the screens are made. A good sense of intuition comes from experience. Paying attention to detail at every step of the process – including things like colour tinting and paper handling – make the difference between an average printer and a good printer.

Kid Icarus

opposite page:
Dolly Demoratti at
Mother Drucker Berlin,
washing a screen with
a pressure hose

Exposing the screen

This process uses a simple photochemical reaction to burn your design onto the screen. Where the UV light from your light source hits the coated screen, that area of emulsion becomes hard. The part it doesn't hit – the part covered over by your design – remains water soluble. You rinse out the emulsion to create your stencil.

The cheapest option is to use the sun as your source of UV light, although it is hard to be precise with exposure time. Another option is buying or building an exposure unit with incorporated UV lights and, ideally, a vacuum blanket. Here we will consider a generic mid-range DIY set-up.

Checklist

○ coated screen
○ film positive
○ blackout
○ UV lights
○ sheet of glass
○ stopwatch
○ exposure unit

Sandwich

Make a sort of sandwich: first the glass (so the film is pressed evenly); then the film positive (avoid mirroring it); then the screen, print side down; and finally, the blackout to keep out unwanted light.

Blackout

The blackout could be as simple as a foam square inside a black t-shirt, slightly bigger than the squeegee side of the screen. Tuck it into the squeegee side; it will fill the whole space snugly.

Expose the screen

Put the lights on and start the stopwatch. As a rule of thumb, exposing less will give you a screen that reproduces finer detail well but doesn't last as long. Exposing more, meanwhile, gives you a thicker and thus more durable screen, but loses finer detail.

Exposure time test

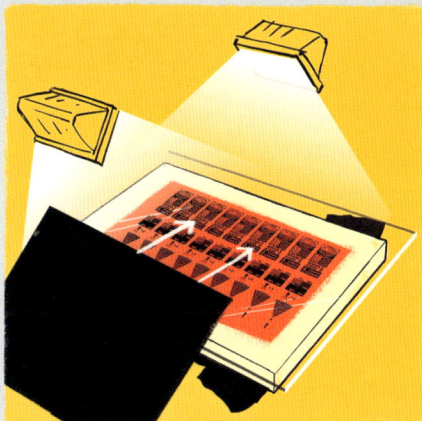

Exposure time test

A good way to find the ideal exposure time is to test your set-up with an exposure card.

Once you have your sandwich, place a piece of card between the light and the image, covering the whole image. Turn on the lights.

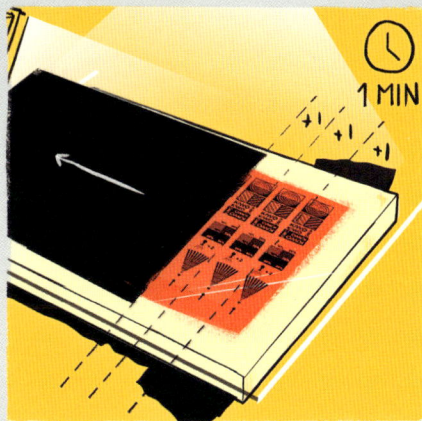

Slide the card

At certain intervals (every minute, for example), slide the piece of card out a few centimetres, exposing another strip of the screen to the lights.

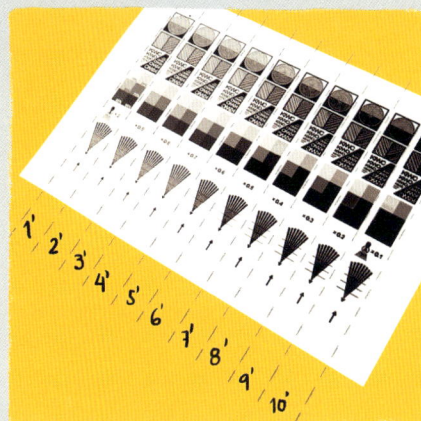

Evaluate the test

Once you have pulled the piece of card all the way out, you will have a screen that at one end is under-exposed, and at the other is massively overexposed, with the whole spectrum in between. Print a print, find the sweet spot and then shoot for that time when you burn your screen for real.

— The screen creates a connection between the digital and physical art realms, letting you move fluidly between traditional painting and digital collage.
Michelle Miller

Silkscreen Masters

Rinse screen

Turn off the lights after the right amount of time has elapsed. The screen is like a cake that carries on cooking after you take it out of the oven, so wash it out at once. First, give both sides a good rinse.

Reveal design

Reveal the design with the pressure hose. As the emulsion washes away, you will see your image emerge.

Check

Hold the screen up to the light. Anywhere light comes through, ink will come through.

Retouching

Imperfections in the mesh or film positive can leave tiny holes. Alternatively, overexposure or uneven coating can mean the emulsion doesn't wash out so well on some details.

opposite page:
retouching the screen
before printing at
Hansiebdruckerei Kreuzberg

Retouching II

If they aren't too close to the design, patch them up with a paintbrush and a dab of emulsion. Put it back under the lights.

If the detail didn't wash out so well, you can blast it with the hose and, if necessary, patch it up.

Post-hardening

'Post-hardening' your screen after you wash out the design increases the stencil's strength and longevity. This involves leaving your screen on the exposure unit for some extra time while the photo emulsion cures hard.

Tape off screen

Now tape off all 'open mesh', or those parts of the screen that you don't need. First, place a piece of tape along one edge of the print side of the screen.

Climb the sides

Making sure that the tape climbs up the sides of the frame in this way will ensure that no ink slips through the tiny gap between the tape and the edge of the frame.

Cover all open mesh

Carry on, moving inwards in a kind of spiral, until the whole print side of the screen is taped off, barring a rectangle in the middle with the design in it.

Tape coins

If you don't have a print table, here goes a good trick: tape a coin to each corner of the print side of the screen.

Ensure bounce

The mesh shouldn't touch the substrate directly: the ink should only hit the page when you apply pressure to the screen with the squeegee.

The coins raise the screen enough for it to have the necessary 'bounce'.

opposite page:
Clare Halifax screen printing with only some small portions of the screen

Sylvia Tournerie
ESADHaR

Angèle Lejof
Le Phare

parcours
de design graphique
contemporain
9 mai au 29 juin
2017

Atelier Banquise
Maison de
l'Étudiant

Kiblind
Le Tetris

...lieu Roquet
...Roue Libre
...Lycée Saint-
...ncent de Paul

Printing

5

Screen 'printing' is a misleading term, in the sense that you spend little time actually printing, and a lot of time getting ready to print. The printing process is the fruit of long preparation, and the success or failure of your eventual print run depends on how thorough you have been in the pre-printing stage.

That said, the moment of printing is when you can be at your most virtuoso, and your creativity can flow most freely. Once the basics have become a reflex, there are few restrictions on where you can take silkscreen, or on where it can take you.

But let's get those basics locked down. In this chapter, we will see first of all how to print with one colour, and then how to scale up that operation to print with two or more colours. And we'll start by looking at how you print onto paper, and then see how the process differs when you print on textile.

opposite page:
large format multicolour
print by Ralph Schraivogel,
screen printed at
the renowned Lézard
Graphique studio
in France, 2017

I always recommend that people start by printing black on white – you get good results quite quickly, and you don't need to worry about registration. Then move on to white on black, so you have to pass twice. After that, a pre-mixed, standard tone. And from there, start experimenting.
Matze, Siebdruck-Corner

Printing one colour

It's a good idea to master single colour printing before you move on to more complex designs. Once registration has become second nature, and your squeegee technique is burned into your muscle memory, you will be ready to tackle anything.

Precision and organization are key, no matter how many colours you are using. It will be easier for you to print well at a more complex level if you adhere to these values from the start.

Checklist

○ a screen with the stencil
  burned onto it
○ open mesh blocked out with
  tape
○ a squeegee
○ ink, properly prepared
○ substrate, properly prepared
○ registration tabs (for paper)
○ any chemicals you may need
○ a spatula

Fix screen

First thing is to attach your screen as firmly as possible to your printing surface. The screen should not be touching the paper directly, but will need a bit of bounce.

Attach film positive

Lightly tape your film positive to a piece of paper in exactly the place you want the print to be.

You are going to line this up with the screen itself.

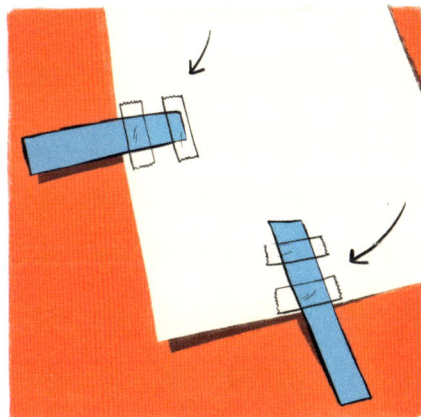

Make arms

Cut out two 'arms' from long strips of paper and attach them to the back of the paper, so that they extend about 10 cm from the middle of a long side and a short side of the sheet.

above:
printer Dolly Demoratti
holds up a film positive
at Mother Drucker

Make sure your clamps are tight and don't shift. I sometimes draw a pencil line on the table at the corners of my screen so I can spot any shift. I always use three points to register to, and keep the two points on the longest edge of the paper as far from each other as possible.
Kid Icarus

Sweet spot

Place piece of paper plus film positive under the screen. Lower the screen. Now use the arms to manipulate the sheet of paper, and line up the film positive with the image on the screen itself.

Registration tabs

Raise the screen, and place registration tabs. You can make tabs out of rectangles of discarded acetate and double-sided tape. Stick two of them directly onto the printing surface at two points on a longer edge of the sheet, and at one point on a shorter edge.

Place paper

Line up a piece of paper so it fits perfectly with the tabs. Lower the screen.

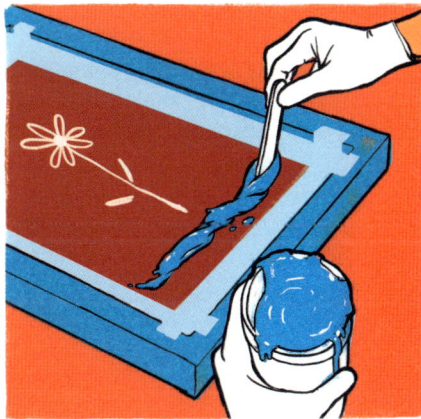

Ink goes in

Pour or scoop the ink into the screen between the image and you, a few centimetres below it.

Put too much, it will get messy and the ink may dry, but it is better to have too much than too little on the screen.

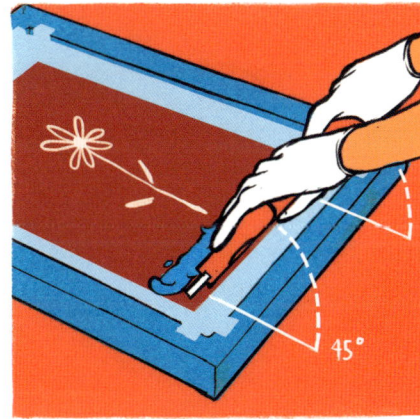

Flood stroke

The flood stroke covers the screen with ink. This ink 'floods' the screen, and it is this ink that will hit the substrate when you apply the print stroke. Do not apply too much pressure: the mesh should not touch the substrate with this stroke. Hold the squeegee at about a 45° angle.

Flood

Slide the ink away from you across the part of the screen to be printed, so you cover it over with a layer of ink.

Print stroke

Now you are going to pull the ink towards you across the screen, this time applying pressure. Using both hands, place the squeegee between you and the ink at about a 45° angle. Apply firm, even pressure as you pull: the screen will make a satisfying whistling noise when you get it right.

Ink hits paper

The pressure will push the flooded ink onto the substrate.

Remove print

There goes your first print (like with pancakes, the first is often not that good). Lean the squeegee against the edge and lift the screen. Remove substrate and put it to dry.

Repeat

Replace substrate. Lower screen. Add more ink if necessary. Repeat.

Recover ink

Once you've finished your print run, scoop as much ink as possible back into the container.

Done

If you are printing with just one colour, that's you done. If you are printing with more than one colour, follow the following steps.

opposite page:
multicolour test prints
from Design & Other, 2017

Printing multiple colours

Printing in more than one colour involves the exact same process, except that you will use multiple screens to successively print on the same substrate.

Registration becomes even more important. You are not just making sure that each print is in the same place, but that each colour lines up.

You have prepared a separate screen for each of the different colour layers. As a rule, you should print the lightest colour first, and the darkest last.

Second colour screen

Put in place your second screen, corresponding to the second colour to be printed.

Attach film positive

This time you are going to tape the film positive of the second colour onto the print you just made.

Line them up carefully

Make sure the film positive and the first print are perfectly aligned.

Sweet spot

First, remove the registration tabs from the first run. Then, as before, attach 'arms' to the back of the print and line it up under the new screen.

New registration tabs

Attach new registration tabs.

Place paper

Line up a piece of paper so it fits perfectly with the tabs. Lower the screen.

Multiple colours on a single screen (taping)

One possibility for printing multiple colours with one screen is to simply tape off those parts that you aren't printing with.

New tabs

Imagine you are going to print the image above in two colours. For the first print, you cover the heart over with tape, and only print the words.

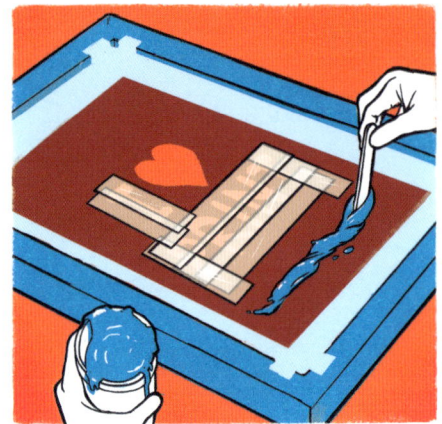

Print new colour

The second print is vice versa: tape over the words, and only print the red heart with the second colour.

Multiple colours on a single screen (Rainbow)

Another way to get several colours out of one screen is to make use of an imprecise but impactful rainbow effect.

Apply inks

Apply two or more different colours where you would normally place only one.

Print

Print as normal. Check the result: if one ink is overwhelming the other one, or if one is edged out by the other over the course of several prints, simply add more ink.

opposite page:
Tind using the same
screen and printing with
two colours at a time

Printing on textile

We have explored the basic mechanism of silk-screen as it is applied to printing on paper. Now we're going to look at how to adapt that mechanism to printing on textiles.

The major difference between paper and textile is actually at the design phase. You will need to make sure that your design works with textile, and the substrate and mesh you choose are the correct ones.

Glue in place

It can be useful to have some sort of wood board to lay your t-shirt flat, and separate it from the back. Put it into position and spray it with glue so it stays there.

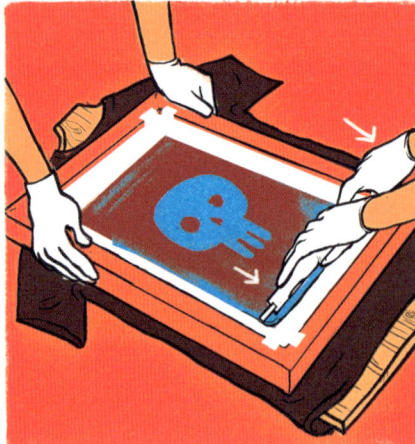

Place design

Hold down the screen and place the design at the desired distance from the neckline.

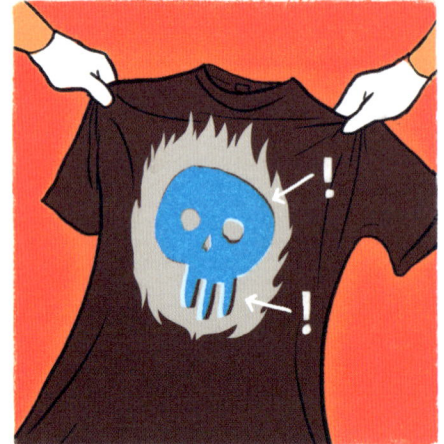

Registration on textile

Printing multiple colours on textiles without a carousel can get messy. The elasticity of the material makes it hard to have a consistent frame of reference. You can adapt the method you use to print on paper.

Printing with a carousel

As with a print table, a carousel is a very smart buy if you want to print at any scale beyond the purely domestic. Of course, it represents a quite significant investment, but you will never look back.

There are a whole range of carousels, from domestic set-ups to industrial machinery. Here, we're going to look at the core process. Of course, you will need to adapt this to your particular machine, and learn its ins and outs and inexplicable idiosyncracies.

Checklist

o t-shirt
o spray glue
o screen
o inks

Find position on shirt

Start by laying your shirt or garment flat on a table (easier than directly on the carousel). If using more then one size, take a middle size. Tape transparency where you want the print to hit. Measure from the neckline to your design: this will stay the same across all different sizes.

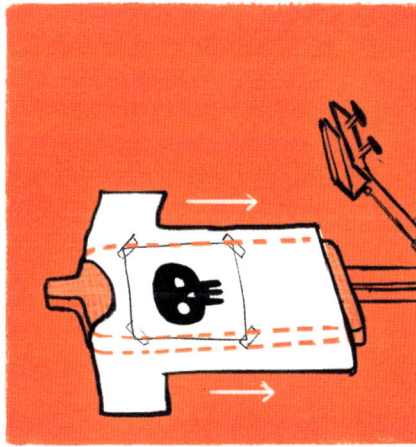

Load shirt

Load this shirt onto a print board on one arm of the carousel. Your shirts will always be loaded onto the board the same way.

Register screen

Attach the screen in the clamps on your carousel. Most carousels allow you to alter the position once the screen is in the clamps. Pull down the screen and line it up with the shirt.

Silkscreen Masters

Double check

To make doubly sure you're happy with the positioning of your image, do the previous steps in reverse: use the screen to define where you attach the stencil, then remove and lay it flat. Test all the different sizes you have.

Multiple colours

When printing with multiple colours, you can load all the screens onto carousel arms at the start, and find the positioning of each successive layer using the position of the first layer.

Fix it

You can use spray glue to fix the textile to the surface. This is essential if your colours need to be hit twice, or if you are printing multiple layers.

Print

Most printers have their own routine which they adapt. A common one is to flood with the screen up, and then pull towards you with the screen down. Another option is to pass twice, with the squeegee at the same angle. Some people like to flood towards them, and then print pushing away.

Multiple colours

Different set ups require different steps. On some carousels, the screens spin and the print boards stay stationary; on others, it's the other way round. The number of arms you have defines how many colours you can print at one go.

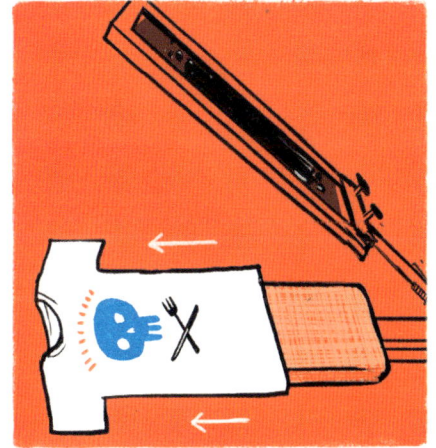

Dry

Once you have printed all the colours you want to print, simply take the shirt from the screen and leave it to dry (see next section).

opposite page:
close up of puff
inks on textiles at
Siebdruck-Corner

I think for new printers the biggest challenge is giving yourself enough time to make a ton of work that is all experimental. That's the only way to learn the process, perfect your printmaking, and then create the imagery you really want.
Michelle Miller

It may sound cold, but as a printmaker I try a little to be like a machine: I try to mechanize the gesture, to limit and control the few determinant variables. At the same time, I am not a machine, and I'll never be able to get that result in that way. The best I can do is try to obtain a human version of machine work, which is slightly but fundamentally different. The core principles of my practice as a printer may be found in this slight difference.
Andrea Baldelli from Corpoc

My personal approach to screen printing is very much about improvising directly at the printing table. I decide everything very spontaneously, for example the colours I use, how many times I use the screen in one print-run, how I flip the paper while printing, and so on.
Thomas Kühnen

I love watching the image slowly come to life as you add each layer. I love mixing the colours and the moment a blurry vision of colour from your mind comes to life in medium and paint before you. And also the tactile quality of a print – being able to feel layers of ink sitting on the paper. It makes a welcome break from the untouchable colours on the computer screen.
Laurie Hastings

Post-print

6

Printers often emphasise that their practice is not linear – they don't simply take on one job, complete it, and move on to the next. Rather, they are at the centre of a network of feedback loops, with each job forming part of a broader continuum. As your practice gets more streamlined and your processes slicker, the planned and the random start coming together in dialectical harmony.

Thus you are never strictly 'post' or 'pre' print. There are, however, a few bits of best practice that you should follow after a print run winds up. Reclaiming a screen properly is a most essential skill. Order and cleanliness are fundamental at every step of the way, but become particularly important in the space between jobs, as mess tends to snowball.

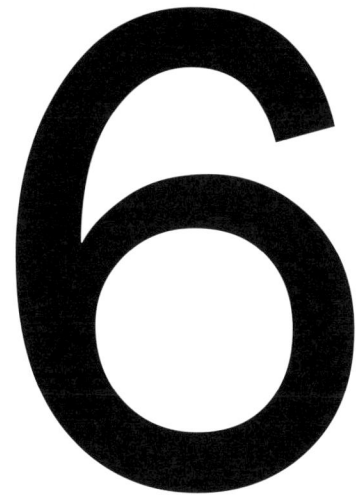

opposite page:
the washout booth at
Mother Drucker Berlin, a
work of art in its own right

Drying and curing

Done with printing, it's time to leave your prints or t-shirts to dry. A slapdash set-up can lead to ruined prints and general chaos.

So, while hanging up or laying out your prints to dry gets the job done, this will become unsatisfactory as a solution as you expand, and you will want to invest in a drying rack.

And, while some ink dries naturally on fabrics, other inks need to be cured with heat to fix them.

Hang

Hang prints to dry. Keep away from dust, wind, infants.

Iron/heat gun

You can iron your shirt to fix the ink. A more professional solution is a heat gun, which doesn't come into contact with the ink. A flash dryer is used for professional finishing.

Flash dryer

A flash dryer is a good thing to have. It can be attached in place of a screen on the carousel itself, or it can have its own mobile stand. It allows you to dry/cure ink between layers, and avoid ink contaminating the underside of neighbouring screens.

Clean-up

It is highly recommended that you clean the ink off your screen as quickly as possible after you finish printing. If you leave it too long, it will dry and clog the pores of the mesh, rendering it unserviceable.

Checklist

○ detergent
○ sponge
○ water
○ power hose

Wet

Use a hose to wet the screen and wash off as much ink as possible.

Soap

Apply household detergent to the screen using a sponge. You can be fairly liberal.

Scrub

Using the sponge, work the detergent into the screen. Then rinse off detergent and ink using the hose.

Reclaiming a screen

Treated properly, screens can be reused numerous times. To prepare a screen for a new image, all the emulsion needs to be washed off, and the screen properly cleaned. This process is called reclaiming.

It's a good idea to get reclaiming done straight after your print run finishes. The sooner you do, the easier it is to remove the emulsion, and the less wear and tear the mesh will see.

Checklist

○ used screen
○ emulsion remover
○ sponge
○ latex gloves
○ ghost remover

Wet

Wet both sides. As always, a pressure hose makes your life much easier. If it is particularly heavily stained with ink, you may want to get it out first with ink degradent.

Work

Spray emulsion remover onto both sides and then work it in with a sponge or brush. Be careful not to scratch or rip the screen.

Scrub

Let it sit for a minute or two, but not so long that the chemical dries. Then with the sponge gently remove the softened emulsion.

A good printer must have an appreciation of the process. The ability to think in layers, to understand colour in terms of overlaid inks. Attention to detail, without losing sight of the bigger image, the larger idea. **Jeffrey Dell**

Blast

Blast both sides with your pressure hose. Spray from bottom to top so you don't sluice off the chemicals.

Ghosts

Sometimes your screen gets ink hazes or 'ghosts'. Hold it up to the light: if light can't pass through, it will show up next time you use that screen. To remove ghosts there is a special chemical known as ghost remover.

— I've worked in this industry for 22 years. It took me three and a half years to understand the basics. Then I started learning. I still learn something new every day.
Niko from Siebdruck-Corner

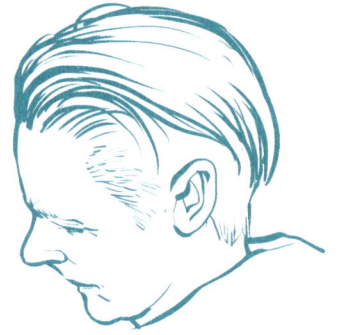

— Take other people's advice and experience with a grain of salt. Nothing is impossible in silkscreen until you've decided it is. People will always tell you what you can and cannot do, but that is based on their own experience. Some of the coolest things I've done, I did to prove someone wrong. I constantly try things I know won't work. But 'won't work' is relative: things that won't work for this design can open a door for a future one.
Daniel Barros

There are infinite possibilities in screen printing. There is endless potential for compositions and relationships between shapes and colours, textures and flats laying together and creating different energies on a page. All of these energies and potential compositions exist within the matrix of the silkscreen before you pull the squeegee.
Michelle Miller

I'm more an artist than a printer. I think printing methods have to be an art form and not just a reproductive technique.
Zansky

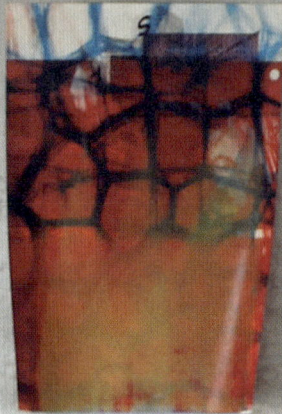

Silkscreen masters

So you're on top of the basics. You've set up a space and filled it with tools and materials. You've got the hang of designing for silkscreen, and by now have prepared enough screens to feel confident doing it. You've printed a range of designs onto different substrates, and are comfortable wielding squeegee and spatula.

One thing that you may have noticed is that there is often more than one way to go about things. What we have covered so far in this book has been a straightforward, one-size-fits-all approach to screen printing. But in reality there are as many ways to screen print as there are screen printers. Now it is time to elaborate your workflow, and define your own personal practice in line with your needs, limitations, and ambitions.

In this section, we will showcase the work of a selection of printers, artists, studios, and other people who form part of the screen print ecosystem. Our selection is, of course, highly personal, but was made with the goal of showing a wide range of approaches, and focusing on specific aspects of the practice of innovators, pioneers, and scene-leading printers. In the following pages you will find material and words that we hope will inspire and inform your own practice, as well as confirm your sense of the truly limitless potential of this artform.

opposite page:
exhibition view of a
selection of test prints
by Thomas Kühnen

Modern Multiples

Dubbed the 'West Coast Warhol', Richard Duardo (1952–2014) was a prolific figure in the Los Angeles underground. He founded Modern Multiples, his Factory, in 1999, the culmination of a succession of silkscreen studios and art hubs.

opposite:
Richard Duardo at
Modern Multiples

Modern Multiples
—
Richard Duardo
Hendrix, 2003

below:
Richard Duardo,
Robert Berman, and
Keith Haring in 1984

Artist, master printmaker, publisher, dealer, gallerist, and collector, Duardo was the original multihyphenate. A self-proclaimed 'third generation Pop Artist', he set up his first screen print studio in 1977, with the backing of a local nun. Over the course of his career, he came to work with artists as prominent as David Hockney, Keith Haring, and John Van Hamersveld. Alongside this, he worked tirelessly at a community level, nurturing the careers of generation after generation of emerging artists and designers.

Duardo's own work featured portraits of icons like Jimi Hendrix, Duke Ellington, and Che Guevara, many of them produced on a one-arm screen printing press, in what he characterized as "a mash-up of street art and high art." He would often add hand-finished pastel touches to the final piece.

Richard Duardo brought people together. Modern Multiples became a focus of the fine art print world, connecting artists from many different movements and subcultures, in meetings that would sometimes spark parties lasting days. Artists like Banksy, Frank Romero, Shepard Fairey, John Valadez, and Retna teamed up with Duardo and his staff to produce images found in collections all over the world. Duardo's legacy lives on at Modern Multiples, today a hub in the world print scene, producing museum-quality screen prints and archival pigment editions for artists.

top:
Modern Multiples
—
Banksy
Applause, 2006

above:
Modern Multiples
—
Frank Romero
*Arrest of the
Paleteros*, 2010
32-colour screenprint

below:
Modern Multiples
—
Richard Duardo
Dylan, 2003
hand-painted
screenprint

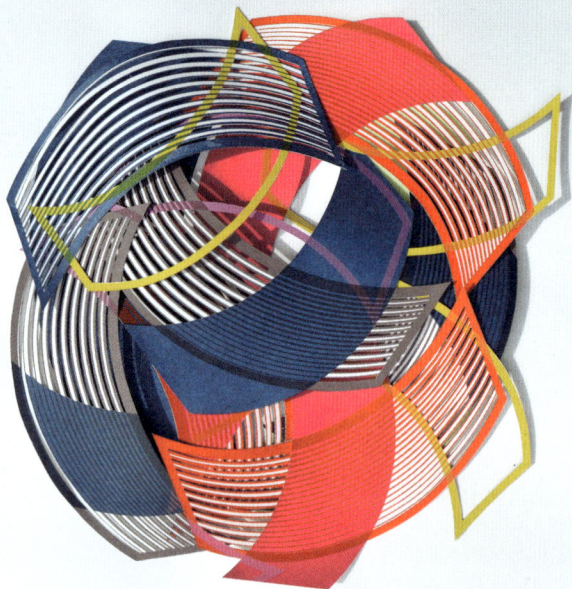

left:
Design & Other
—
Tier I (Fountain Fountain series), 2013

opposite page:
Design & Other
—
Gelati Columns
(In Giro series), 2011

below left:
Design & Other
—
Moss Covered Northern Lights (In Giro series), 2011

below right:
Design & Other
—
Döner Carpets
(In Giro series), 2011

ROME · ITALY

ROMA · ITALIA

D&O

CAM + MON 12/15

Mother Drucker

From a modest operation, the Mother Drucker screen print studio has grown to become a focus for the Berlin silkscreen community, as well as an important reference point in the global scene.

opposite page:
Dolly Demoratti at Mother
Drucker with a detail of
Oskar Rink's *Rot*, a 17-colour
print produced for the
Circle Culture Gallery

this page:
the interior of Mother Drucker,
including the print archive
and screen storage space

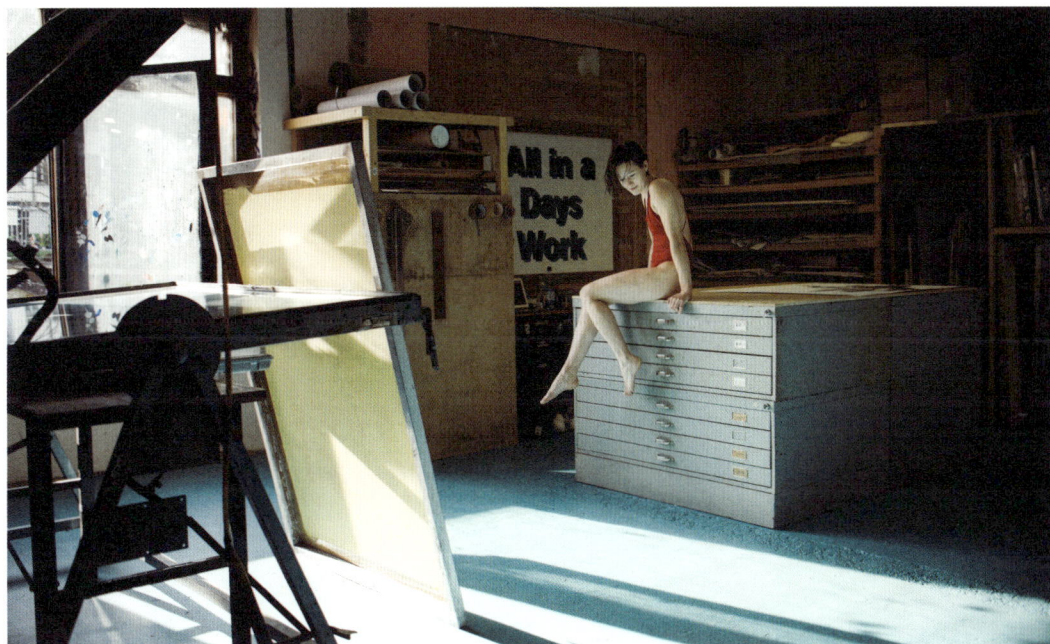

Mother Drucker was founded in 2010 by Londoner Dolly Demoratti. Run out of a Kreuzberg shopfront, the project served as both a studio and a gallery space. Out of it grew, in August 2011, the city's first ever festival of print, Druck Berlin. Comprising three eclectic days of printing and exhibitions, the festival's goal was to provide a platform for learning and involvement, bringing together people from the screen print community and the world at large. There have since been two further equally successful instalments.

right:
the second Druck Berlin
Screen Print Festival in
full swing ran from 6th
to 22nd December, 2013,
at the Stattbad, a 1960s
swimming pool complex;
shown are some prints
by Alias in production,
in the print studio
installed in the pool

above:
Dolly hanging a
large format print
by L'Atlas inside
the Mother Drucker
studio produced for
Urban Spree in 2016

opposite page:
CYMK print with
additional layers and
hand-finishing, part of
a series documenting
tattoo culture

In 2012, Dolly moved Mother Drucker to bigger premises at Urban Spree. This unique space is at the heart of Berlin's alternative art scene, and Mother Drucker is an integral part of it. Urban Spree is defined by a collaborative ethos that Mother Drucker in many ways shares. From the outset the studio has worked hard to bring people to screen printing and screen printing to people, not least through Druck Berlin, as well as different series of workshops and tutorials.

It was at Urban Spree that Mother Drucker consolidated its reputation as a specialist in high-quality, large-format silkscreen print on paper, gaining a respected clientele list and creating editions with many top artists. After only ten years in the industry, Dolly has worked with Aguirre Schwarz (Zevs), Victor Ash, and Tavar Zawacki (Above), among many others.

Recently, Mother Drucker has been expanding, opening a sister organization called Backstage Printing, an apparel printing company.

Studio focus

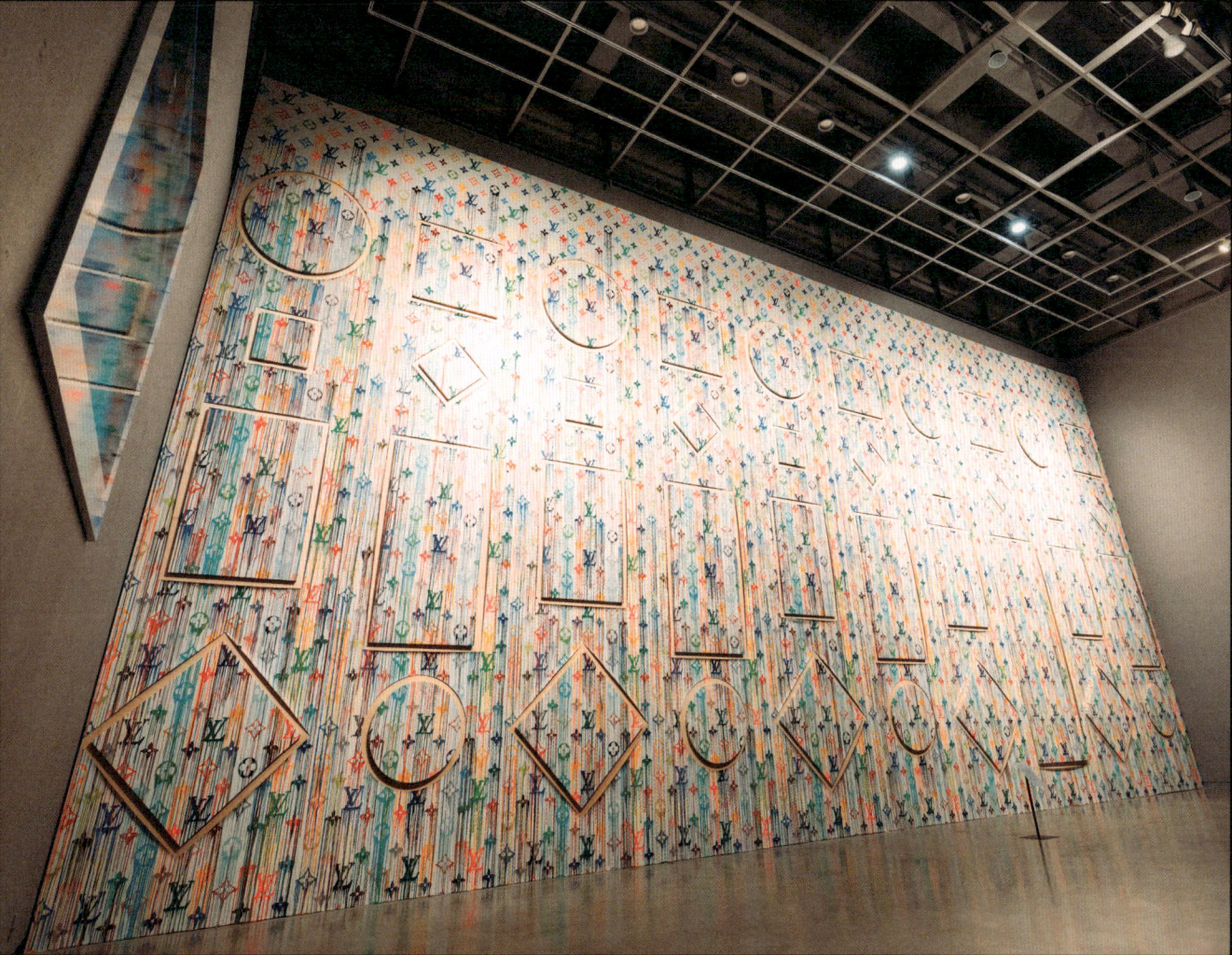

This awe-inspiring project is the creation of acclaimed French street artist Aguirre Schwarz (a.k.a. Zevz). The goal was to cover a huge wall with strips of canvas, each of them screen printed with a pattern made up of the Louis Vuitton logo repeated thousands of times. Aguirre's trademark 'liquidation' dripped paint effect was then applied to each one.

The wall – at the National Museum of Calligraphy in Seoul – was 16 m by 8 m in size. Led by master printer Dolly Demorati, the team printed 10 strips of canvas, each strip 1.6 m by 10 m. In total, the design featured 23 colours, and the screen printing process required 4320 individual pulls.

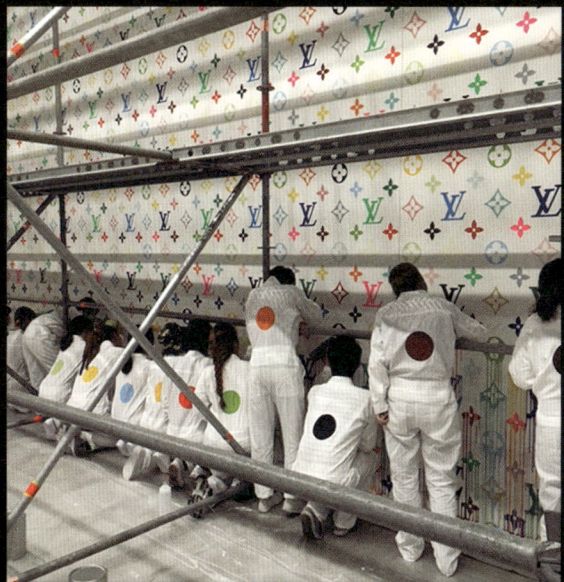

Medulla

Medulla, based in the Italian city of Modena, is the creation of artist Davide Montorsi. Here he explains a little of his philosophy, and how he came to be a trailblazer in creating and using 100% organic inks.

Printing ecologically is the logical next step after eating ecologically: most people don't realize that all day, every day, their body is in contact with unhealthy, environmentally damaging fabrics.

opposite page and above: Davide Montorsi in his studio, creating and printing with his range of totally natural inks, from preparation to use

"I believe that every action, including printing, should be guided by deep thought. When Goethe visited Italy and saw the botanical gardens at the Palace of Caserta, he came to the conclusion that nothing in nature is random, that every plant is shaped the way it is for a reason. I think the same idea should be applied to screen printing. Your technique as a printer needs to develop in line with your needs and inspiration. My goal was to develop a zero-impact colour, based on natural pigments.

To make a completely natural colour I went back to basics: Cennino Cennini's *Il libro dell'arte*, a manual written in the Middle Ages that serves as a kind of recipe book for making art, starting from raw materials, including colours. After this, I spent a whole year experimenting intensively.

Working with natural pigments isn't like opening a paint shop. Each colour functions in a different way, from extraction to application, with different times and seasons. The variables multiply exponentially. New attempts are made based on previous errors, until you can a make a totally natural colour, without chemical catalysts, that stays on the screen and won't come off in the washing machine. It took me a year.

If you want to start experimenting with natural pigments, you need to have a quasi-Zen approach, and come to screen printing with a more meditative, more organic perspective. Bear in mind that, with traditional screen printing, we think about ink drying in time intervals that range from five minutes to two days, depending on the inks used. With natural colours, this interval increases to two weeks, and sometimes even two months."

above:
Medulla
—
Luca Zamoc
Poster for Node Festival, 2016
5-colour screen print, with three greys made of graphite and two blacks made from a mix of chlorophyll extract, rubia and indigo dye

left:
Medulla
—
Poster for Borgo Indie, 2014
3-colour screen print with ink made from chlorophyll extract and indigo dye

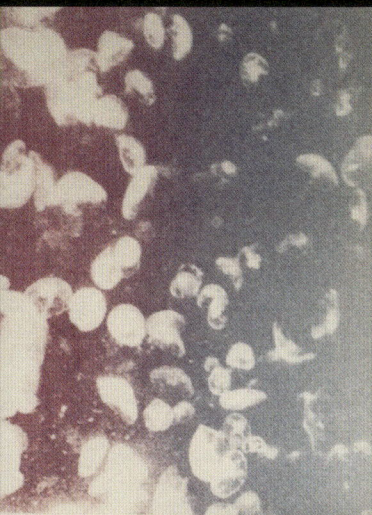

My father is a dyer in Japan. He started his career using the Yuzen technique to dye kimonos, but later began working with natural dyes. I wanted to print with non-toxic materials and colours from nature, using materials I had to hand. At first I used egg as medium, just like in fresco painting. Then I experimented with different adhesives, and finally hit on rice paste as the perfect base medium. You can print on anything, but being water-based, the ink can wash away quite easily. The ink has to be made fresh, so forget about conserving it. And the colour can vary every time, so you have to accept what you get.
Chika Ito

left:
at work in the studio at
Harvey Lloyd Screens

below and opposite page:
Harvey Lloyd Screens
—
Stephen Wilson
Shine On, 2017
created to support
Refuge, helping Women
and Children suffering
domestic violence

following spread:
Harvey Lloyd Screens
—
Mr Bingo
Advent Calendar, 2017
this alternative
calendar features a
gold layer which can
be scratched away to
reveal naked people

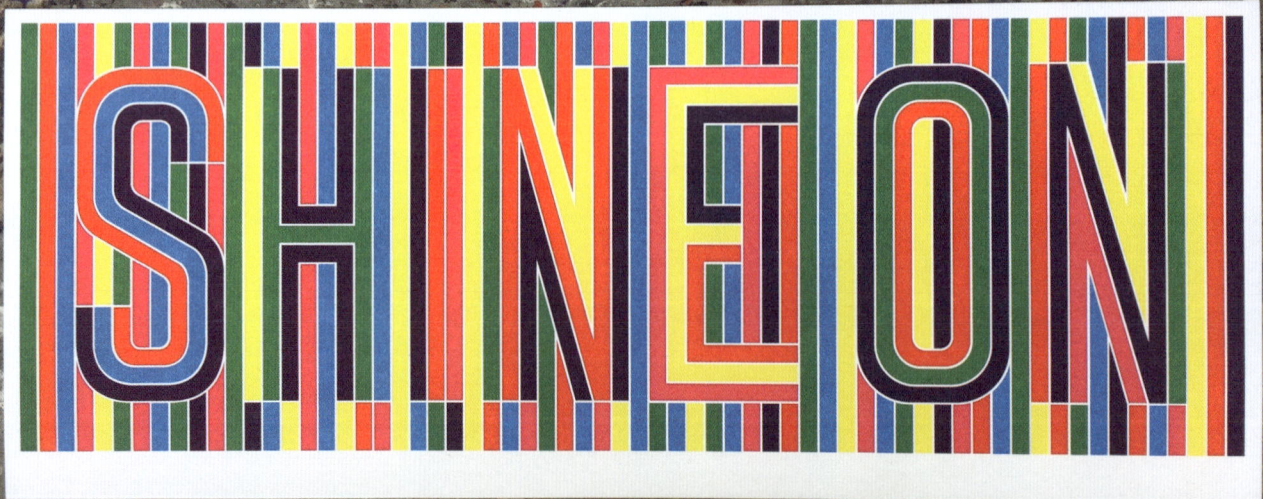

left and below:
some details of invitations
printed by Sara de Bondt
at Harvey Lloyd Screens
with iron filings on card

IF YOU COULD
KEEP ONLY ONE
MEMORY WHAT
WOULD IT BE?

We have printed iron filings on card invites and had
to work out a way to make the card rust. We have
printed cement on paper for a series of Limited
Edition prints. We have printed inks that glow in
the dark and inks that are invisible during the day
and then light up during the night.
Harvey Lloyd Screens

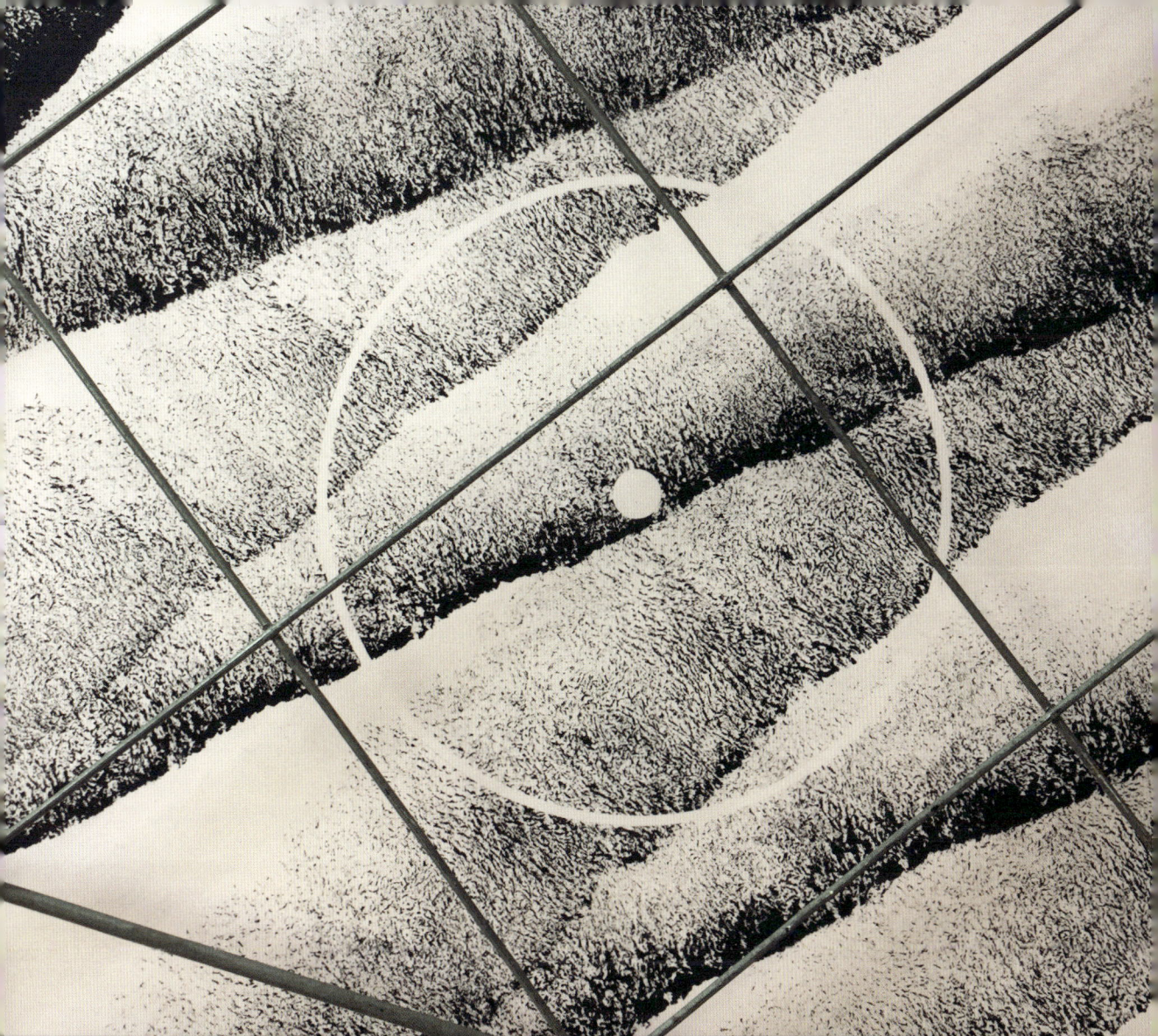

above and left:
Harvey Lloyd Screens
—
Spin, n.d.
different pieces from
the same print series

Below:
Harvey Lloyd Screens
—
Adrian Johnson
Lion, 2017

opposite page and above:
Harvey Lloyd Screens
—
Damien Poulain
*She Lights Up the
Night*, 2017

left:
Harvey Lloyd Screens
—
Anthony Burril
Noon 2 (detail), 2017

DAMIEN POULAIN

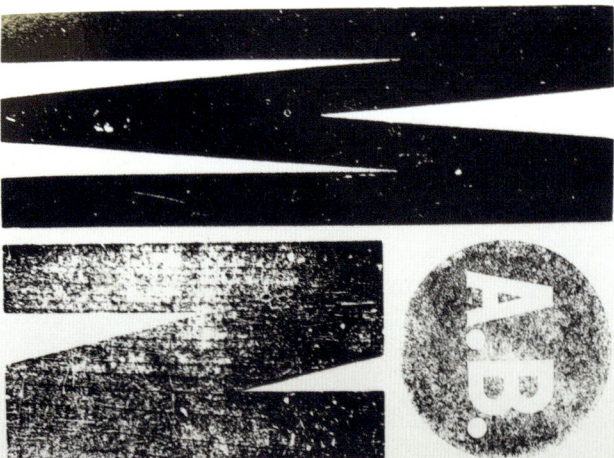

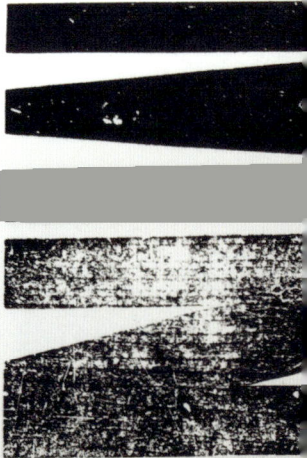

A.B.

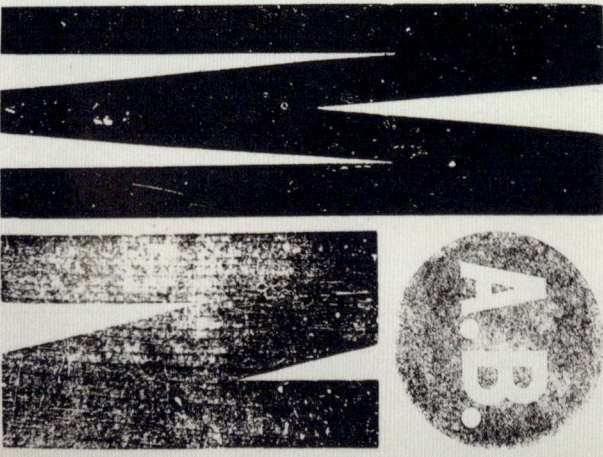

A.B.

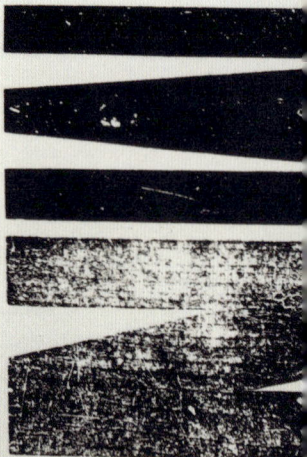

A.B.

above right:
Harvey Lloyd Screens
—
Adrian Johnson
Draw A Line 1, 2016

above left:
Harvey Lloyd Screens
—
Adrian Johnson
Draw A Line 2, 2016

left:
Print About Me
—
Business Card, 2013
screen-printed brick

When you design for silkscreen, you get to think about the product very deeply. I think about the texture I want, the contrast against the base I picked. I can be precise in the colouring, in the opacity of the colours, I can orient the printer in so many different ways. And, while we often use machines, it feels very much like an artisanal process. The challenge is always finding the right quality to print on. Scarves, for example, sometimes feature very transparent bases, which allows me to push the colour to the other side and make it a perfect double-side print. But if I am using a special textured ink or puff, it will shrink and mark the fabric. It takes experimentation and a lot of respect for the technique.
Daniel Barros

right:
Daniel Barros
—
scarf design for
Kenzo, 2017

Siebdruck-Corner

The world of screen printing offers a lot of opportunities for specialization. We were welcomed into Siebdruck-Corner by Niko and Matze to find out more about sourcing and supplying high quality inks, as well as how to remesh screens.

Berlin has a rich tradition of printing, and today the city boasts a vibrant print ecosystem, bringing together printers, studios, suppliers and galleries. For silkscreen enthusiasts, a vital element of that ecosystem is Siebdruck-Corner, a store that provides a wide range of high quality inks, from classic colours to a panoply of special effects.

Founded by Niko in 2014 as an outgrowth of the Siebdruckservice Schiller print studio, Siebdruck-Corner sells ink all around Germany and Europe. A cornerstone of their mission is sustainability, which is one of the reasons they are such vocal advocates of water-based inks. As Niko's colleague Matze puts it, there is almost nothing you can't do with water-based inks; the resistance to them in some quarters is really just a hangover from a time when solvent-based inks were the only viable option for medium to large-scale printing. But there have been many advances since those days, and water-based inks are often the smartest option, not least for environmental reasons (bear in mind, however, that in Berlin the temperature never reaches the sort of tropical heat that can make water-based ink impractical).

The quality of their products is testament to the commitment and vision of the Siebdruck-Corner team. "This isn't just a job," Niko says. "It's a passion."

opposite page and above:
remeshing screens at
Siebdruck-Corner

right:
some of the range
of inks on sale

opposite page:
Re:Surgo!
—
Blanquet, Gfeller,
Hellsgård book
collaboration, 2014

left:
Taller 57
—
Zosen
Untitled, n.d.

below:
Thomas Khünen
—
books, 2017

I print for myself and chose to print intuitively, generally using it as a paint medium rather than a facsimile process. I embrace all the flaws, textures and inclusions. I want you to see my hand in the making of the piece.

Lorenz Boegli

Lorenz Boegli is a magician with materials, master of a range of mesmerizing effects. His approach is both highly philosophical and rigorously scientific, giving his prints a uniquely numinous quality.

"My research has been in the direction of halftone effects with iridescent pigments or pigments which are normally used for cosmetics. My engagement with printing with light reflective inks has resulted in the innovation of RGB print, for which I have applied for a patent. For the first time, red, green and blue, printed on black material, overprinted white."

Dedicated to his craft, Boegli plays with metallic and iridescent reflections, blending lustrous and matt finishes, and combining them into half-tones. Silkscreen offers him, he says, the broadest possible palette of enhancement effects (most of which simply do not photograph). As he himself puts it, "screen printing in the year 2017 is still the most creative and innovative printing technology of all. It's THE effect printing system, because nearly all effects need big pigments and screen printing is the only printing technology that can deposit them."

And, since 1997, Lorenz Boegli has been developing a series of paper products adapted to silkscreen. Examples include the Schuhgelenkpappe series, made of material normally used for insulating shoe soles, or the prizewinning 'carnets nature'.

opposite page:
Lorenz Boegli at work
in his studio

above:
a photo of the presentation
card he sent to agree to
talk to us for this book

right:
a detail of the cover Boegli
screen-printed for the book
Pasang, or, *The motherland
is worth more than the
kingdom of heaven*

Above:
Clare Halifax
—
Look It's London, n.d.

Left:
Clare Halifax
—
London at Length, n.d
6 colour screen print

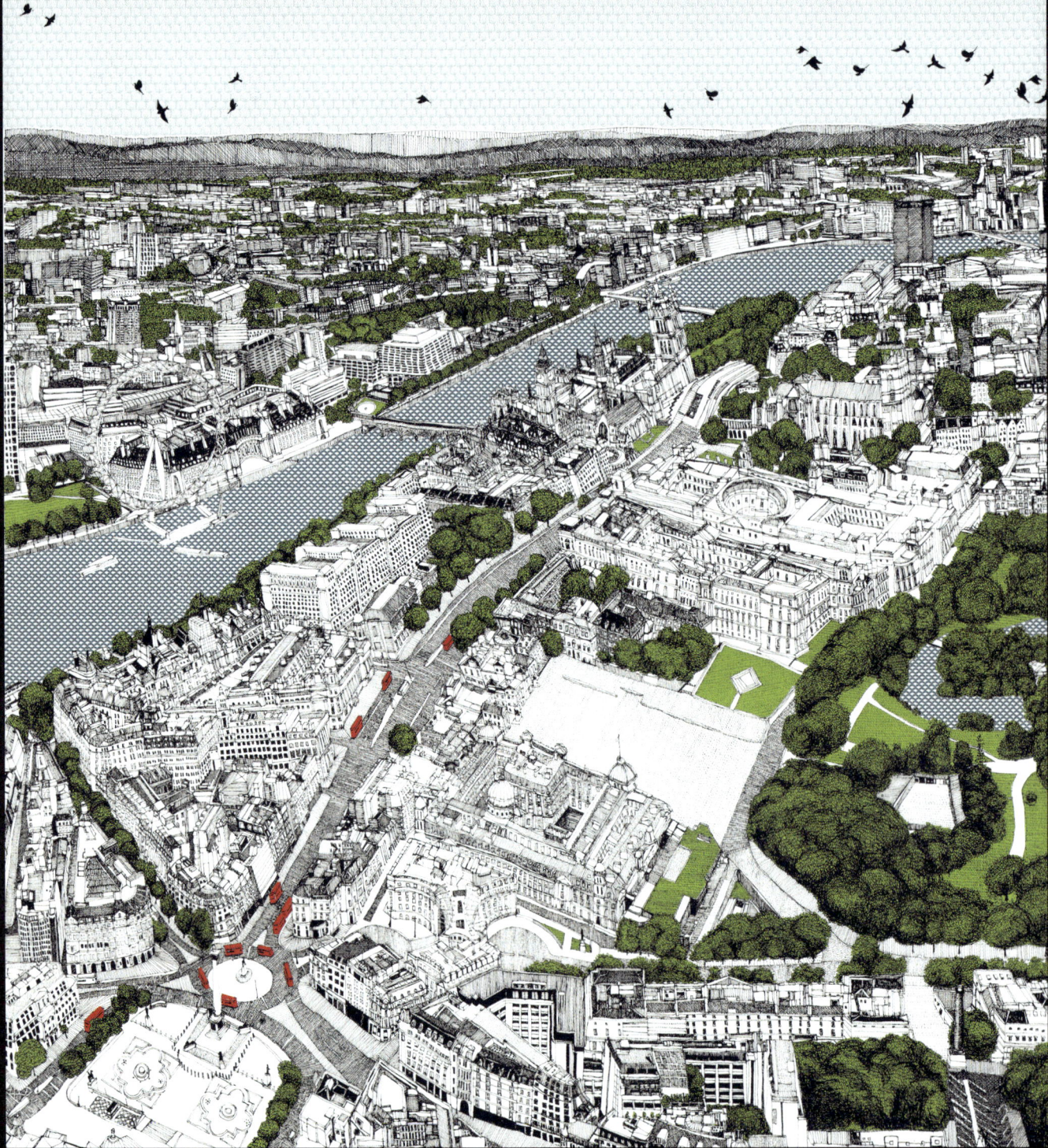

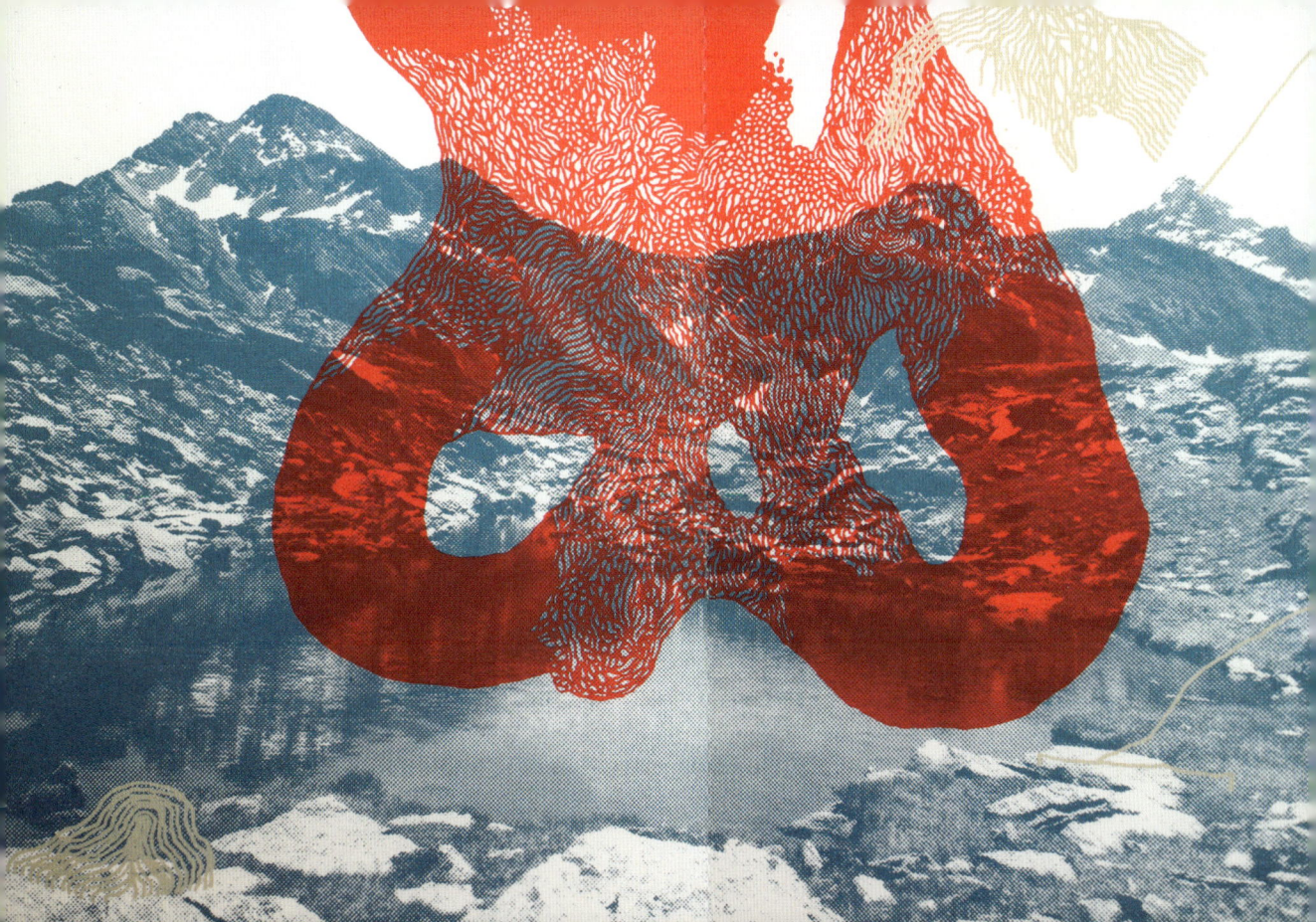

bove:

Print About Me

08 *PENN*, 2014
LEGS n° 1, from the
series LLEGS, leporello
books, design by
Print About Me

ight:

e Dernier Cri

érôme Minard
pread from *Second
Porte*, 2017

above and top:
Print About Me
—
Bread Benischek
60 Yards, 2015
the artist and Paolo
Berra printing 60 yards
of denim at Gowanus
Print Lab, Brooklyn, NY,
photo by F. Cirilli

right:
Paolo Berra's print
studio, 2016
(Print About Me
workshop)

left:
Print About Me
—
Philip Giordano
*The Day I Became
A Woman*, 2012

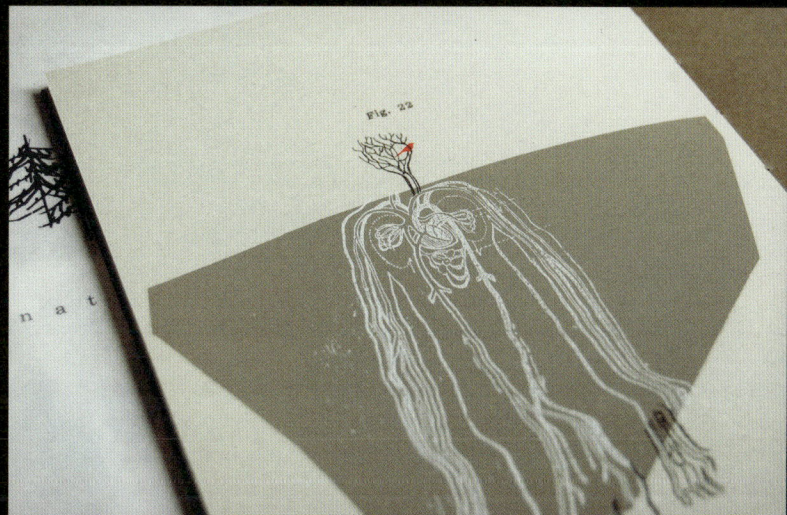

above left:
Print About Me
—
Daniele Catalli
*Del Lavoro & Della
Morte*, 2013
13 cards for the 13
most dangerous
professions in the EU,
photo by Moisi Guga

above right:
Print About Me
—
Paolo Berra
Di Natura Stupida, 2011

right:
Print About Me
—
108
PENN, 2014
printing LLEGS n° 1,
from the series LLEGS,
leporello books, design

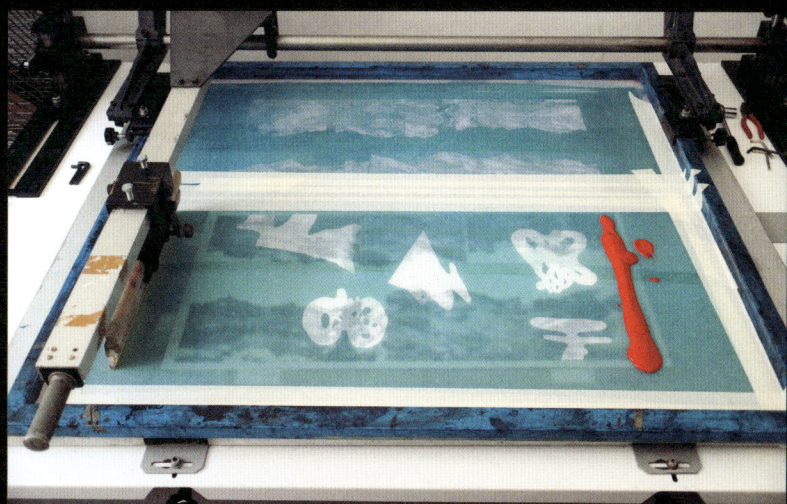

opposite page:
Print About Me
—
Sophie Lécuyer
À Mon Seul Désire, 2013,
photo by Moisi Guga

above and top:
Print About Me
—
Elisa Talentino
Le Jardin d'Hiver, 2013
9-colour screen print,
photo by F. Busso

right:
Print About Me
—
*La Print About
Machine*, 2015
human-powered screen
printing machine

Melanie Yugo

Melanie Yugo is the director of Possible Worlds, a gallery and project space in Ottawa, Canada, which opened in 2015 as part of the Spins & Needles project. She shared with us some insights into her socially-engaged print philosophy.

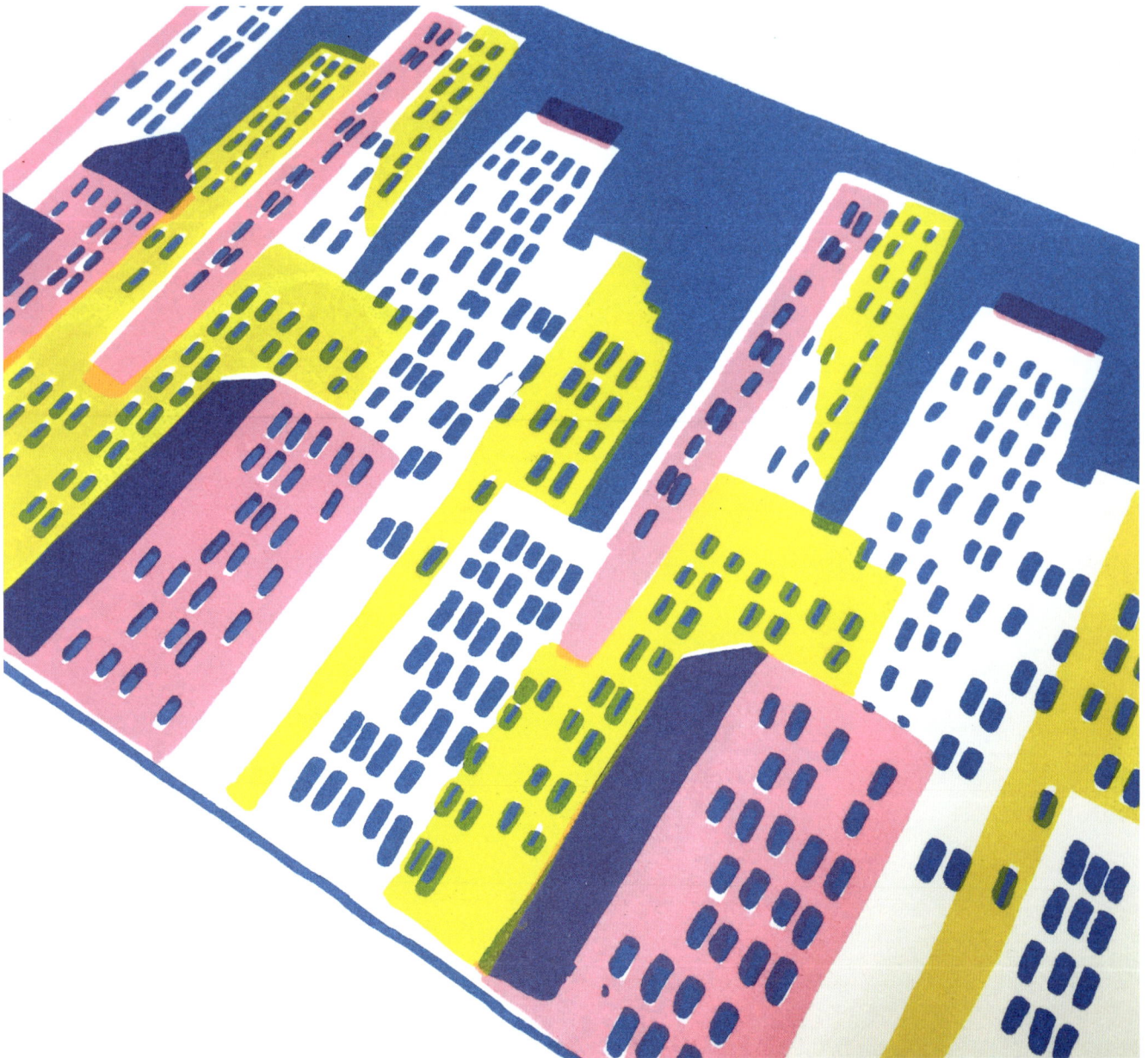

"As a print artist, I specialize in silkscreen and Risograph printing. My own work, in the form of prints and artist books, explore themes of community, culture, identity and place. Silkscreen is one of several tools and processes I use in my socially-engaged art practice. Alongside writing, teaching, publishing, research, and organizing exhibitions, my artistic interventions are centred on the development of inclusive, experimental platforms that promote and share under-represented perspectives and practices. Possible Worlds, which I co-founded and co-direct, brings together these activities.

I situate my print and publishing work within the context of graphic art and its ability to be democratically available to a wide diversity of publics. Silkscreen can allow for relatively inexpensive and sustainable experimentation. In taking the form of multiples, such as prints or artist books, printed matter becomes a platform which can contribute to broader critical discussions.

My workflow goes back and forth between being defined and making it up as I go along. Because of the nature of silkscreen, which I do by hand, I have learned to embrace good planning and serendipity at the same time. When I get down to printing, it gets very instinctual. I tend to put together colours or shapes or images or lines slightly different than from what I planned. The hands-on aspect of printing often affects my end result. Often I am very ambitious about printing when I first generate ideas, but when I start putting the squeegee to paper, the print takes a life of its own. Even the simplest shapes and colours silkscreened together can result in unexpected surprises and combinations."

above:
Melanie Yugo
—
Everyone's a Winner Baby (detail), 2014

left:
Melanie Yugo
—
Noodle Bowl, 2015

opposite page:
Melanie Yugo
—
Experiments in City Life (detail), 2014

Studio focus

One of the biggest challenges I face as a printer is finding space to work and time to create. Having proper space to undertake a project is important, so that you can accommodate the right equipment and have designated areas to increase efficiency in your work. Making sure I balance my own personal printmaking work with commissions, teaching, and my other art initiatives is also a challenge. Part of my printmaking creation process requires a lot of focus and discovery, and sometimes this can be neglected when I am working on other things.
Melanie Yugo

I borrow ideas from other ways of making images. Glazing techniques in painting, for instance, taught me I could do something similar in screen printing with ink layers that are 99% transparent, with just a hint of colour and value. I believe my work pushes screen printing a bit closer to things like painting and, to a certain extent, what is happening in photography today. **Jeffrey Dell**

above:
Jeffrey Dell
—
Midsummer Century, 2016

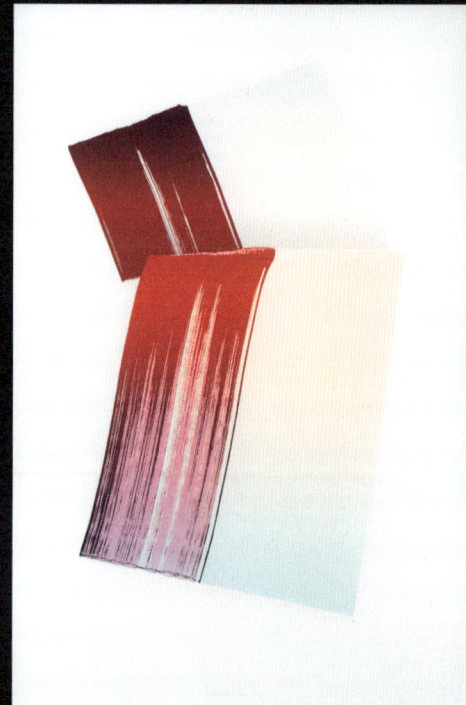

left:
Jeffrey Dell
—
Dreamland II, 2015

opposite page:
Jeffrey Dell
—
The Site 2, 2015

I've been making prints long enough that most of my ideas come in the form of prints, as opposed to images generally. The ideas are intrinsic to how a particular film positive will expose to the screen, how I can print layers on top of each other to achieve a particular effect, to what happens to a dimensional form when it's printed with a contradictory gradient. The ideas are really linked to how the image is going to be constructed through printing.
Jeffrey Dell

far left:
Jeffrey Dell
—
High Wasted or Waisted 1,
2012

left:
Jeffrey Dell
—
*Little Baller Machine
(with sprinkles),* 2012

opposite page, lower right:
Jeffrey Dell
—
Second Moonbeast, 2016

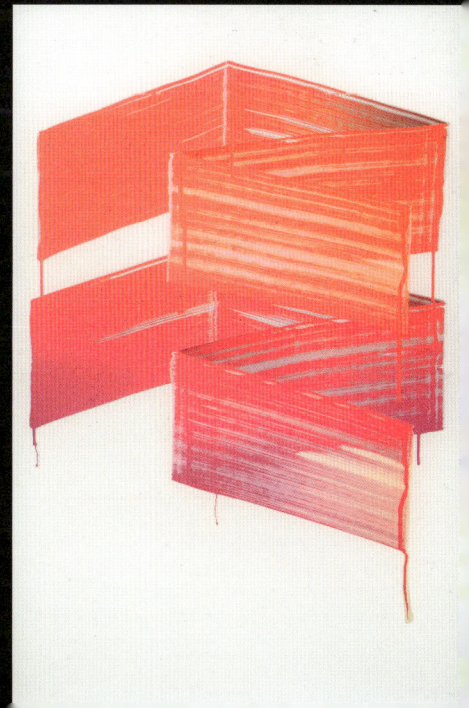

I generally start each print with a basic pencil drawing, but no colour. I'll have an idea of what should happen with the colours, but really this is made up as I go along. I'll sometimes reprint a layer to modify the colour, so I'm really discovering it more than simply executing a pre-designed image.
Jeffrey Dell

Harwood King

Founded by artist Quentin Best in the 1980s, Harwood King is a group of print artisans based near Brighton, UK, with a decades-long track record of producing fine art prints. We invited Quentin to share some of the history of Harwood King, as well as his vision of the future for printmaking.

"Harwood King was started at a time when the artwork was hand-drawn, using combinations of pen, brush, and air brush to create an opaque separation onto acetate. Traditional CMYK reproduction wasn't suitable for fine art printmaking: artists tend to use single pigment paints and often create deeply saturated areas of colour, but the colour gamut of CMYK could not reproduce these deep colours. Whereas the human eye can see billions, CMYK printing will only produce around five or six thousand colours. Multicoloured screen printing offered the perfect solution to creating prints with the full colour gamut of an artist's painting. The downside was hand separation and a lot of stencils."

above:
Harwood King
—
Gonkar Gyatso
Buddha on Plastic,
2014
screen-printed on
both sides of an
acrylic sheet, with
gold and silver leaf

opposite page and above:
carefully embellishing *Tiger*
by Dave White with gold
leaf; application takes at
least two hours per print

right:
Harwood King
—
Wayne Warren
Gold Dress, 2014
6 gold colours
and gold leaf

Back in the early 1800s, the invention of photography freed the artist from the need for precise, academic reproduction of their subject. Similarly, today the computer has freed both artist and printmaker from slavishly following traditional methods of production.

"Photographic separations more common in commercial silkscreen printing were often used to help at the early stages of a print. We typically used in excess of 40 colours; for one project 96 separate colours were used on an edition of 500 prints. It took six months to complete. These works had amazing texture thanks to the built up ink, and the prints felt like oil paintings. However, only publishers with deep pockets could afford this type of print publication.

Today, an artwork multiple lets artists share their work with a much wider audience than a single original piece can. The single original will also be unaffordable to many people, whereas a print or multiple can be enjoyed and owned by a range of people. Prints are now so much more accessible, and show a far greater range of styles and production methods; this will only increase as more and more people realize that art prints are affordable.

There is a debate around printmaking nomenclature. It is sometimes claimed that an 'Original Print' has to be produced solely by the artist, creating all stencils and for preference printing it themselves. I disagree. A modern print studio is more akin to a film studio. The artist becomes director, more concerned with content than production. We work as a team with the artist to create a new work. We sometimes take an original as the starting point, but the print develops away from this and becomes a work of art in its own right."

above:
Swimming, a 13-colour print by Howard Hodgkin for the 2012 London Olympic Games; to get the great depth of colour in the dark areas they were printed in layers several times

above:
Harwood King
—

Bonnie and Clyde
Tokyo Beat, 2017
34-colour print with texture,
glitter and sliver leaf

below:
Harwood King
—

Dave White
Frog, 2017
giclée with silkscreen
varnishes and diamond dust

"The future of printmaking is exciting. Inkjet printers, 3D printers, laser cutters and CNC machines have already started to creep into the production of artworks. Computers and digital printing have dramatically cut the cost of producing a print, enabling artists and printmakers to create works together without needing a publisher.

The downside of these new tools is that it is easy to lose the intimate interaction that traditional forms of printmaking give. Traditional printmaking produces accident, which is inherently interesting, in the same way a live music performance can be more exciting than a recorded one. In the blending of new and traditional, the print studio can make a great difference to the artist."

left:
Kate Gibb
—

Abstract Print Girls, 2007
one-off artwork for
Jalouse Magazine,
art direction by Eric Pillault

above:
Kate Gibb
—

Blue Girl, 2017
one-off artwork for
Jalouse Magazine,
art direction by Eric Pillault

opposite page:
Kate Gibb
—

Hockney Boy, 2003
one-off artwork
for the Dries Van
Noten Spring/Summer
Lookbook 2003,
photography by
Ellen Nolan,
styling by Nancy Rhodes

left:
Kate Gibb has created
the sleeve artwork for
many album releases by
the Chemical Brothers;
this print is an unused
sleeve for their
Brotherhood album

opposite page:
Kate Gibb
—
Golden Girl, 2003
one-off artwork
for the Dries Van
Noten Spring/Summer
Lookbook 2003,
photography by
Ellen Nolan,
styling by Nancy Rhodes

My prints are all made intuitively.
I create one-off prints freely on a
table, without registration bars, etc.
That's my approach... un-technical.
Kate Gibb

Michelle Miller

Michelle Miller is a printmaker and painter based in Chicago. Their work consists mainly of large-scale abstract prints, some informed by questions related to queer identity. We invited them to unpack for us some aspects of their process.

"Screen printing is like a second language to me. I try to use printmaking as a form of collage. Through printmaking, I am given opportunities for chance and experimentation, as well as very well-planned and strategically printed pieces. I am able to think about my work through the discovery of what is possible through screen printing. This is important to my creative process and image-making. Being open to occurrences during printing, as well as more controlled experimentations in the form of small mono-printed series, influences and keeps fresh the imagery in my larger, meticulously planned print works."

left:
Michelle Miller
—
Let it Slide, 2017
work in progress

above:
Michelle Miller
—
Party as Form, 2017

I think for new printers, the biggest challenge is giving yourself enough time to make a ton of experimental work.

above:
Michelle Miller
—
Buddha Rays, 2015
31-colour monoprint

below:
tearing paper at Spudnik
Press Cooperative

"I am consistently exploring how the process of screen printing can affect and improve my imagery. Personally, I find flat, consistent layers of ink laid through a silkscreen to be the most satisfying surface quality possible. The uniformity and saturation puts emphasis on the relationships between forms and colours in my work. I try to utilize this as an effective tool for large scale, bold, colourful, minimal prints, and sometimes mono-prints.

I mix all of my own inks from raw pigments and binder. Working with higher quality pigments allows me to mix the vibrant, saturated colours I use in my works. I have found that pre-mixed, store-bought inks have very chalky colours: it's impossible to mix a pure purple or glowing red."

"I personally use Guerra brand pigments, which is an independent pigment company based in Manhattan, New York. Guerra has a line of pure pigments blended with just enough water to be stable as a liquid. I prefer using the 'pigment dispersion' line to pigments in powdered form, both for health and safety reasons, and because it can be incredibly difficult to mix powdered pigment into an acrylic medium. Mixing my own inks also gives me great control over their opacity, transparency, value and tone. My inks and pigments are acrylic, but the effects often end up looking as saturated as oil inks, and are often mistaken for such."

left:
Michelle Miller
—
Hill, 2015

below left:
Michelle Miller
—
Play Thing (detail), 2014

below:
several works by Michelle Miller including *Cloud Shadow* (2016)

above:
Michelle Miller
—
Cloud Shadow, 2016
detail, before framing

A good printer is someone who can truly think through the lens of the medium, much like a composer thinks through an instrument.

Michelle Miller

opposite page:
Tind

Tind

Tind – working with his father at their studio in Athens, Greece – is a legendary figure in contemporary screen printing. With his credo of 'peace, love and silkscreen', Tind has transformed screen printing into a spiritual discipline.

Tind's work bespeaks an explosive creativity. The range of his experiments with ink and substrate (honey and banana leaves, for example), as well as the expressive power of his more conventional projects, have earned him a rightful place at the vanguard of world screen printing. We invited him to share some musings on the role of chance in his practice, and what it means to push the boundaries of printing.

"In the words of Victor Moscoso, 'first it was an accident, then it was by design.' You work with what you have and you learn from it, then you take what you've learned and repeat the process. Eat, sleep, print, repeat.

There is another quote: 'Error is superior to Art.' When you are working beyond the norm, a big chunk of what you do at first seems unorthodox because it leads to no immediate results. But it builds a vast knowledge and understanding of the medium of silkscreen, thus preparing you to overcome any challenges you might encounter in your future endeavours as a printer."

above:
Tind
—
poster for the Syros
International Film
Festival, 2016

opposite page and right:
team Tind at work in the
studio, including a detail of
the *Blessed or Cursed* poster

We decided to do the exact opposite of what you should do when you silkscreen. Normally, when you decide to work with silkscreen, you run an edition and do your best to make sure all the prints look the same. The ultimate goal is to reproduce. But our current practice focuses more on unique works. We play with misprinting, bad registration, and all the things that shouldn't normally happen when you screen print.
Gfeller+Hellsgård

above left:
Gfeller and Hellsgård at
work in their studio

above right:
Gfeller + Hellsgård
—
Grau 2, 2015
silkscreen on wood

left:
Gfeller + Hellsgård
—
Grau 1, 2015
silkscreen on wood

right:
Gfeller + Hellsgård
—
Grau 3, 2015
silkscreen on wood

above left:
Gfeller + Hellsgård
—
Earthrise 2, 2014
silkscreen on wood

above right:
Gfeller + Hellsgård
—
Earthrise 3, 2014
silkscreen on wood

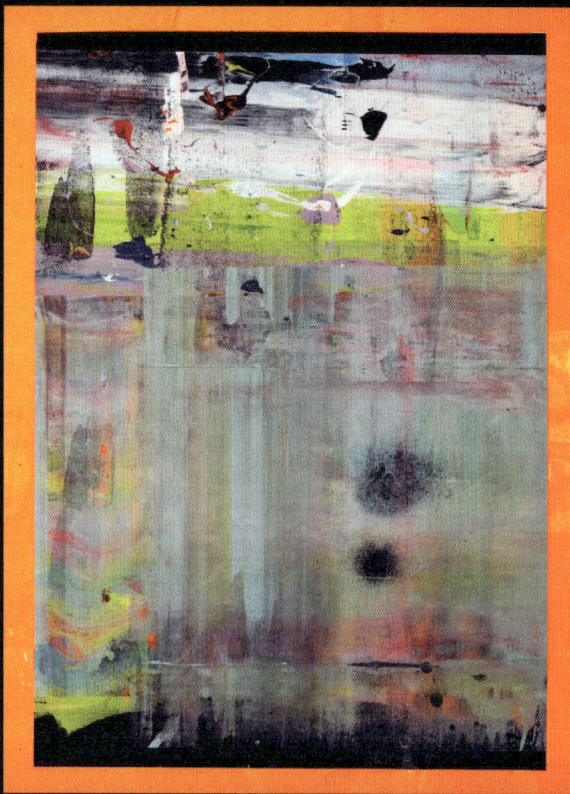

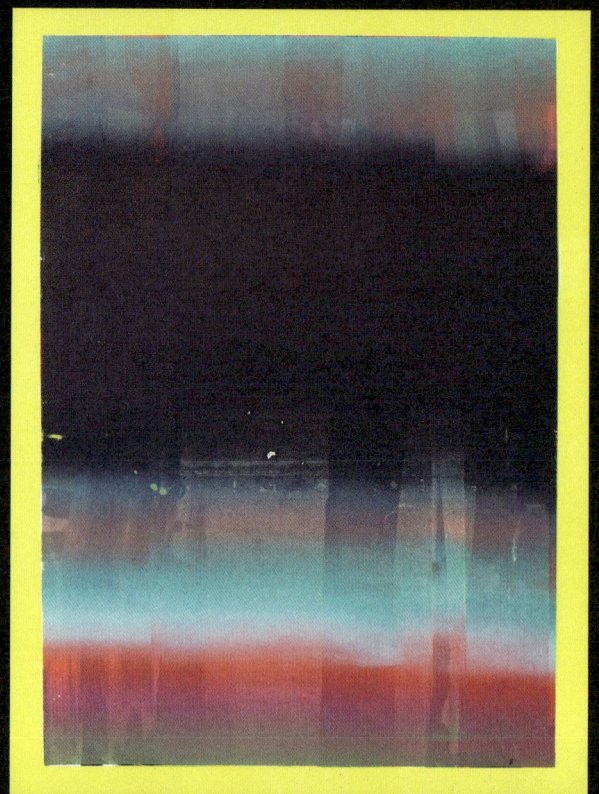

We don't really consider ourselves printmakers. We're probably a printmaker's worst nightmare. What we're doing is painting, but instead of using brushes, we use screens.

Gfeller+Hellsgård

opposite page:
Roland Barth
—
Untitled, 2016

left:
Roland Barth
—
Untitled, 2016

I produce large-format screen prints by sticking paper to a wooden board, which I put on the floor. I do not coat or expose: I use only a blank, uncoated screen, which I paint on directly. The screen works as a media to transfer lots of 'stacked' colour to the paper in one action. By using a screen to print instead of painting directly on the paper, I obtain a complex image with a flat surface. The process of printing like this is defined by planning colours, composition, and orders on the one hand, and on the other, watching and reacting to the results of each step. Chance is an important part of the progress.

Roland Barth

below:
Thomas Khünen
—
Free Jazz Improvisation, 2016

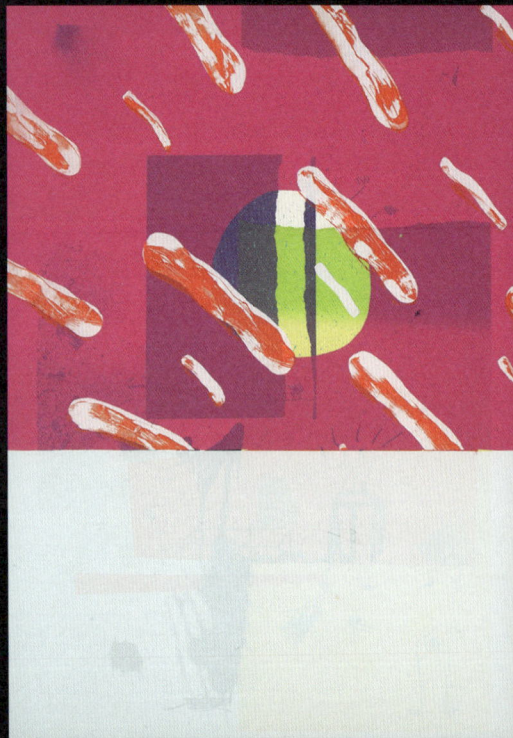

above:
Marion Jdanoff, Damien Tran, Merle Tebbe, and Thomas Kühnen
—
print from Ancien Massiv session, 2016

Marion Jdanoff, Damien
Tran, Merle Tebbe, and
Thomas Kühnen
—
print from Ancien Massiv
session, 2016

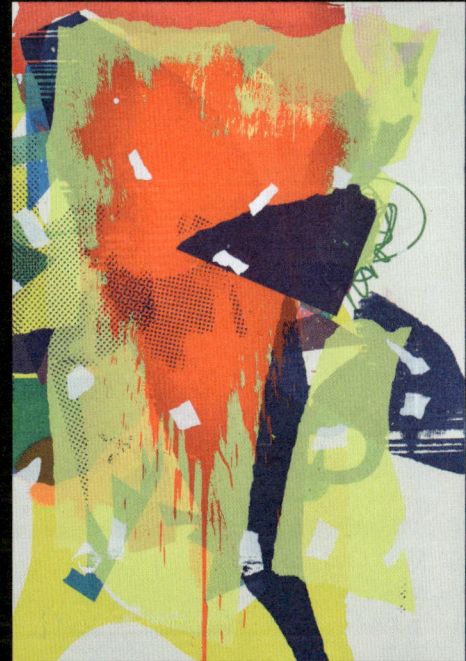

above:
Thomas Khünen
—
Improvisation 28, 2016

left:
Thomas Khünen
—
details of test prints

PAULINE GAVE LE CANCER AVEC LES CHEVEUX QU'ELLE A PERDUS JUSQU'À L'ÉTOUFFER.

PAULINE FOUT LE FEU À LA MAISON DU CANCER. ÇA BRÛLE EXTRÊMEMENT BIEN.

left:
Palefroi
—
Marion Jdanoff and
Damien Tran
*Taper fort, occuper
dur – II*, 2016

left:
Palefroi
—
Marion Jdanoff
spread from the book
Baston, 2016

opposite page:
Palefroi
—
Marion Jdanoff
*Compensation
Carbone*, 2016

above:
Palefroi
—
two pieces from
Pouvoirs, 2016
installation at V9 Gallery,
Warsaw, Poland

left:
Palefroi
—
Marion Jdanoff
spread from the book
Baston, 2016

right:
view of the interior
of the Palefroi studio,
with various completed
pieces on display

below left:
Palefroi
—
Girl Band tour poster, 2016

below right:
Palefroi
—
Le Monstre, 2016

right:

Viadukt

—

Marlene Hausegger
*Beim Warten wird
die Zeit auffällig -
Havanna, 2016*, 2017

left:

Clare Halifax

—

*A Piece of Swiss
Cheese*, 2017

below:

Roland Barth

—

Untitled, 2017

opposite page:
Le Dernier Cri
—
Jiro Ishikawa
image from the book
Chinpoko Jiro, n.d.

right:
Drid Machine
—
DVD Kumlini
Porky, 2016
in collaboration with
Too Strong Looks

left:
shot of a Dernier Cri show,
awash with manic colour
and subversive vibes

left:
Le Dernier Cri
—
Keiichi Tanaami
Death Bridge, 2014

right:
another dense
labyrinth of Dernier
Cri craftmanship

below:
Le Dernier Cri
—
Stan Liquide
Piss Action, 2015

Arrache-toi un oeil!

Paris duo Arrache-toi un oeil! are a colossal presence in the silk-screen poster scene. Their work is a testament of the deep connection between the music industry and screen printing.

below:
detail of an art print
silkscreened by
Arrache-toi un oeil!

Founders Emy Rojas and Gaspard Le Quiniou are designers, illustrators and printers. They started printing under the Arrache-toi name in 2005, and since then have produced hundreds of gig posters, as well as record covers, t-shirts and artists' books. And since 2012, Arrache-toi have worked on a series of remarkable screen-printed installations for festivals and art exhibitions.

Arrache-toi un oeil! create a dense and absorbing visual universe. The eclectic list of Emy Rojas' influences goes some way to explaining the power and distinctiveness of their style: Dürer, Bosch, Alphonse Mucha, Japanese prints, Eugene Grasset, Aubrey Beardsley, Flemish primitives, Pre-Raphaelites, narrative drawings (manga, comics, Charles Burns, Lynd Ward), tattoos, the psychedelic universe of the '60s and '70s, gig posters, manual typography, hand signage, logos, calligraphy...

left:
Arrache-toi un oeil!
—
Converge gig poster, Paris, 2014

below:
Arrache-toi un oeil!
—
Frustration gig poster, Paris, 2013

Our studio is in the 11th district;
pass by to see us if you are in town.

Silkscreen Masters

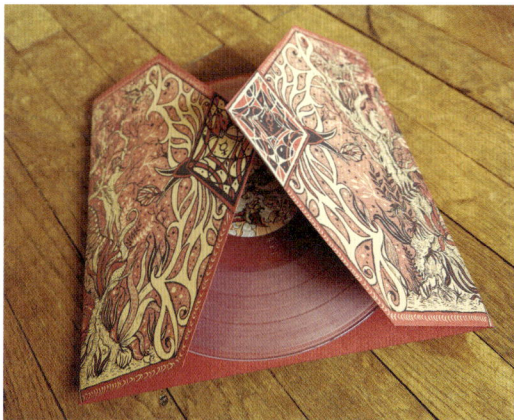

opposite page:
Arrache-toi un oeil!
—
Levitation, 2014
paper and silkscreen
installation

above left and right:
Arrache-toi un oeil!
—
screen-printed sleeve for
Trashley - 'Dance until the
light takes us' EP, 2014

top left:
Arrache-toi un oeil!
—
poster for a concert
organized by Arrache-toi
in Cachan, France, 2013

top right:
Arrache-toi un oeil!
—
Cats, 2017

Studio focus

Freedom is a road
That takes us far, far away
To bring us back home

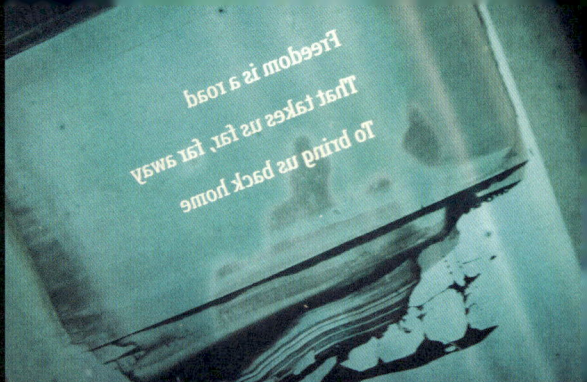

above right and top:
Legno
—
Haiku series of
screenprinted
Moleskine notebooks

right:
Legno at work in a
live screen printing
performance at
the Moleskine
café in Milan

GOOMBAY

MUSIC From BAHAMAS

CHARLIE ADAMSON
BLIND BLAKE
DELBON JOHNSON
VINCENT MARTIN
FREDDIE MUNNINGS
GEORGE SYMONETTE
ANDRÉ TOUSSAINT

1951-59

TRINIDAD GOT
...AMAS GOT
...MBAY !

CHARLIE ADAMSON
BLIND BLAKE
DELBON JOHNSON
VINCENT MARTIN
FREDDIE MUNNINGS
GEORGE SYMONETTE
ANDRÉ TOUSSAINT

CHARLIE ADAMSON

LES DISQUES BONGO JOE
...ACE DES AUGUSTINS, GENEVE, SWITZERLAND

R 002   BONGO JOE

MUSIC From
BAHAMAS

33⅓ rpm

RULE C, A READER

1 AI 2 Art Workers' Coalition 3
ABC No Rio 4 Up Against the Wall
Motherfucker 5 Comité Invisible
6 General Idea 7 Bernadette
Corporation 8 HARD-CORE 9
Critical Art Ensemble 10 Abounaddara
11 Collective Actions 12 subRosa
13 Black Audio Film Collective 14
Artist Placement Group 15 Bureau for
Open Culture 16 DAAR 17 Freee
18 Sankofa Film and Video Collective
19 Group Material 20 BANK 21
Wondrich/Goldsmith 22 Fashion
Moda 23 Dillemuth/Davies/Jacobsen
24 Raqs Media Collective

edited by Atélier Impopulaire

above:
Legno

—

*GOOMBAY! Music from the
Bahamas 1951-59* LP, 2017
Bongo Joe Records

right:
Legno

—

Atélier Impopulaire
Rule C, A Reader, 2017
cover hand-printed
by Legno

above:
Corpoc
—
V3rbo t-shirt, 2013
detail

above left:
Corpoc
—
Luca Barcellona
Untitled, 2016

right:
Corpoc
—
Father Murphy and
Muscle & Marrow tour
poster (detail), 2016
screen-printed with
ink and human blood

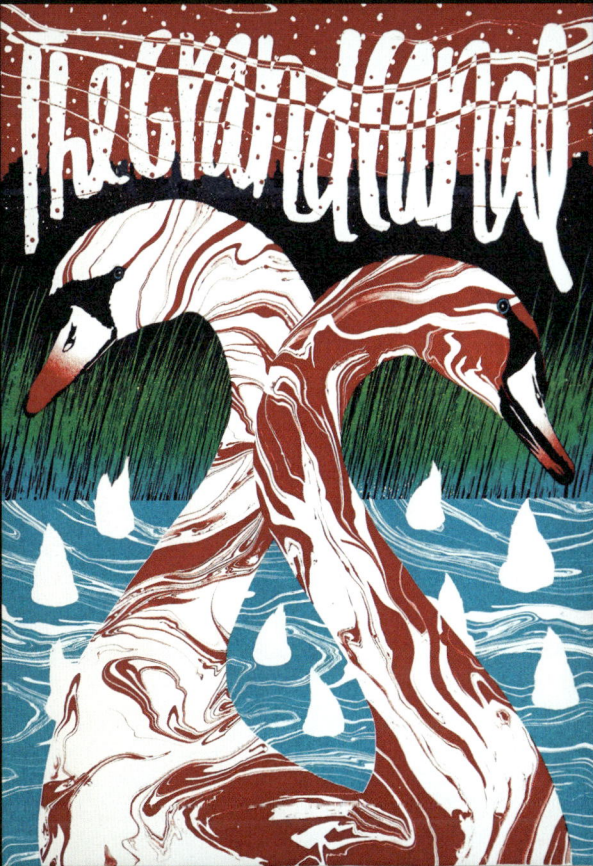

this page:
Dublin studio Damn Fine
Print curated the series *Damn
Fine City* in 2014, inviting
different artists to celebrate
the city in silkscreen;
clockwise from right: Chris
Judge, M&E, Will St. Ledger

Jealous Print Studio

The Jealous studio and gallery set up shop in Shoreditch, London, in 2008, and has carved out a reputation for excellence, printing for artists like Ben Eine or David Shrigley, as well as brands including Tate and All Tomorrow's Parties.

"Being a studio of eight full-time members, there are always a number of projects running at the same time," Adam from Jealous told us. "This means that we have to be very organised in our management of both paid work and our own published work for Jealous Gallery. At any one time, a printer could have three to four jobs that they need to juggle. We try to match each project to a specific member of the team, to find the perfect combination and relationship between printer and artist."

Jealous puts a successful printer/artist relationship at the heart of their practice. In Adam's words: "one of the biggest challenges a printer faces is meeting the expectations of the creative you are working with, and maintaining the artistic integrity of the work. They have entrusted you to produce a work for them, and it is your job to complete that to a very high standard, so they keep on returning and spreading the Jealous name."

Any last tips on ensuring a good relationship with your printer? "Buy us biscuits and we will be your friends forever!"

below left:
Jealous
—
Ben Eine
Celebrate, 2016
featuring Eine's signature Vandal font, this print was made to celebrate the Big Issue's 200 millionth issue

above left:
Charming Barker at work on his *One or Two Cats* print

below:
one of Ben Eine's letter series being printed at Jealous

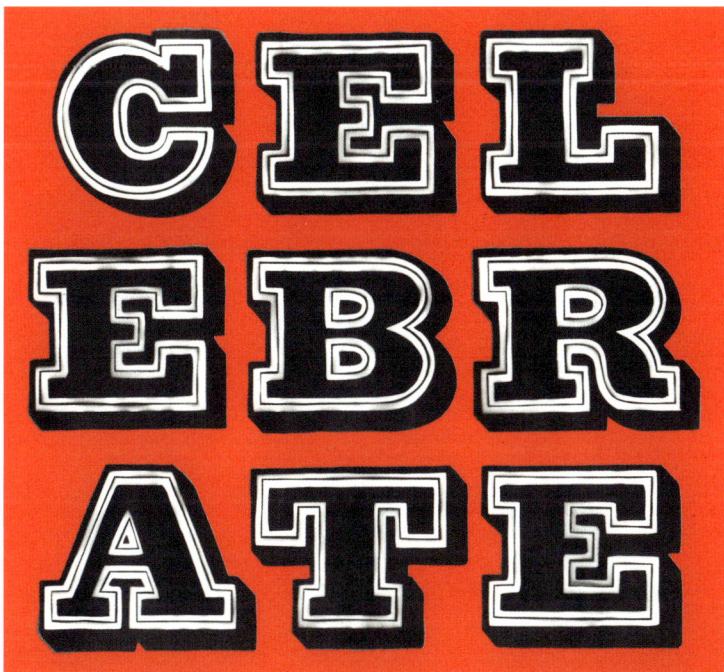

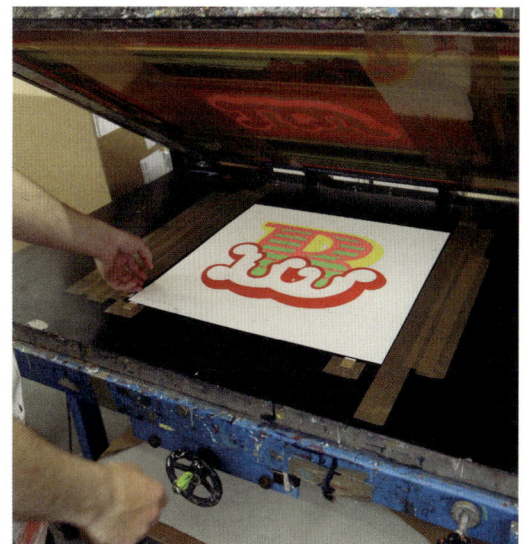

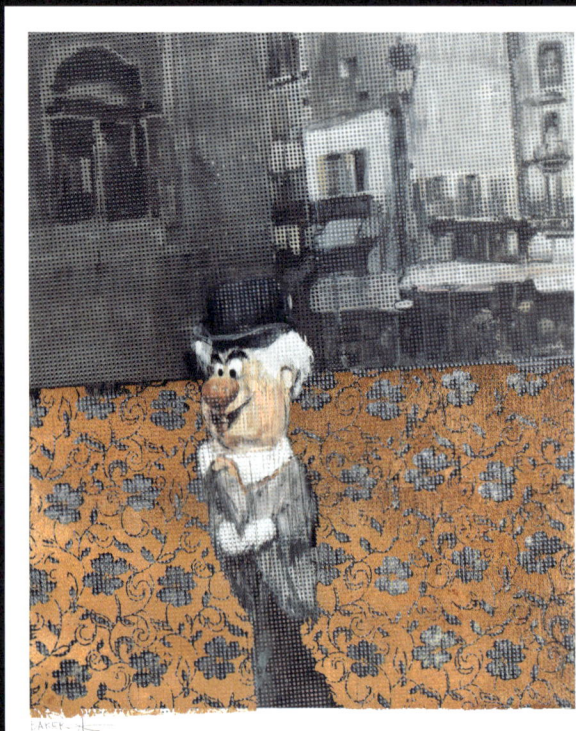

above left:
Jealous
—

Charming Baker
One or Two Cats, 2015
archival inkjet with a
2-colour silkscreen
and varnish overlay,
hand-finished with a
universal wax marker

above right:
Jealous
—

Dave White
Stag IV, 2015
27-colour silkscreen
with white diamond
dust background

left:
Jealous
—

Charming Baker
The Wrong Brave, 2016
archival inkjet with a
2-colour silkscreen
overlay with copper leaf

opposite page:
Jealous
—

Chris Levine
Lightness of Being, 2013

Lézard Graphique

A silkscreen workshop in Brumath, near Strasbourg, France, Lézard Graphique was founded more than 30 years ago by Jean-Yves Grandidier. It is now part of Museum Manufactory, a group that specializes in the creation of innovative exhibition spaces.

Lézard Graphique mainly prints on flat surfaces, focusing on art and advertising posters, signage and visual media. A human-sized company with 12 workers, Lézard Graphique considers itself a workshop more than an art studio. It helps its clients by reworking graphic files and adapting colours, establishing relationships based on commitment and trust.

The team are seasoned technicians, and nothing is left to chance at any stage in the process, from the preparation of the screens to the selection of pigments, or the systematic cleaning of work stations. But Lézard Graphique's reputation does not stem from technical brilliance alone. The workshop displays continual curiosity about experimentation, light, and seeing. In addition, it maintains privileged and lasting relationships with its suppliers of machines, inks and paper.

Believing in mutual enrichment through graphic projects and human relationships, Lézard Graphique remains an atypical entity among an overwhelming majority of offset and digital printing companies. Here, we focus on one project of theirs, a mouth-watering piece by influential Swiss poster designer Ralph Schraivogel.

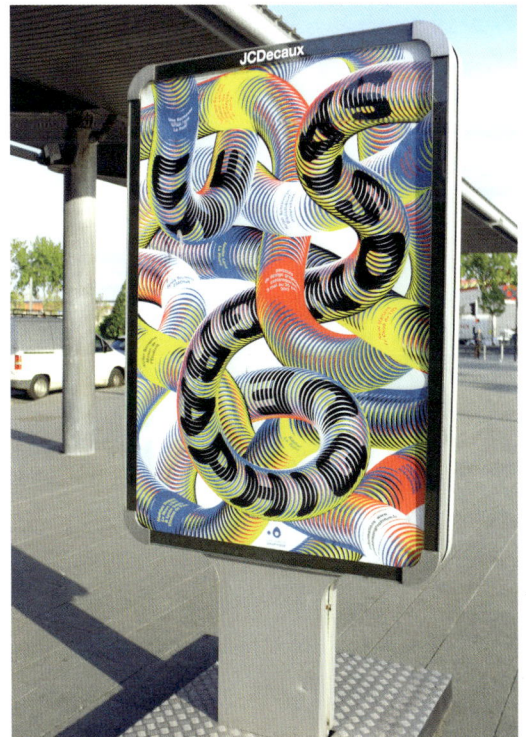

opposite page and above: steps in the process of creating this artwork, from screen to printing (with a view of the Lézard Graphique studio), and finally installation in the city of Le Havre

right:
Lézard Graphique
—
Ralph Schraivogel
Une saison graphique, 2017
Photo by P. Cachard

above left and right:
Strane Dizioni

—

Jesse Jacobs
*By This Shall You
Know Him*, 2011

left:
Le Dernier Cri

—

Keiichi Tanaami
Death Bridge, 2014

opposite page:
Laurie Hastings

—

Birds, 2017

left:
Icinori
—
Planetes Negatif, 2016

above:
Icinori
—
Monde Color, 2016
for Wired Japan

Icinori isn't just our artistic identity, but also an entity devoted to publishing our most experimental and demanding projects. We are passionate about drawing and publishing in every sense. We try to clear our path and our territory step by step. The books we print are simply unreasonable, unchained, and unclassifiable. Their circuit of distribution is very short, and we are involved at every stage, from the first pencil stroke to the printing and binding phases. We like to think of each step of the whole process, from the hand movements when drawing, to inking the screen, as a unique, potentially creative and meaningful act.
Icinori

above:
Icinori
—
Untitled, n.d.

below:
Icinori
—
Factory, n.d.

right:
Icinori
—
Campagne
Strasbourg, 2016

Know your inks. Colour is as important as transparency. There is no colour theory adapted to reality. Use your senses. Never hesitate to stop the printing process and adjust the colour, even if nobody will ever see the difference.
Icinori

Handsiebdruckerei Kreuzberg

Stefan Guzy and Björn Wiede have a reputation for precision that has positioned their studio, Handsiebdruckerei Kreuzberg, at the forefront of the contemporary art print scene. Their practice involves a lot of feedback and interaction between artist and printer, making the finished piece a truly collaborative effort. "We focus more on working with artists than printing," they say.

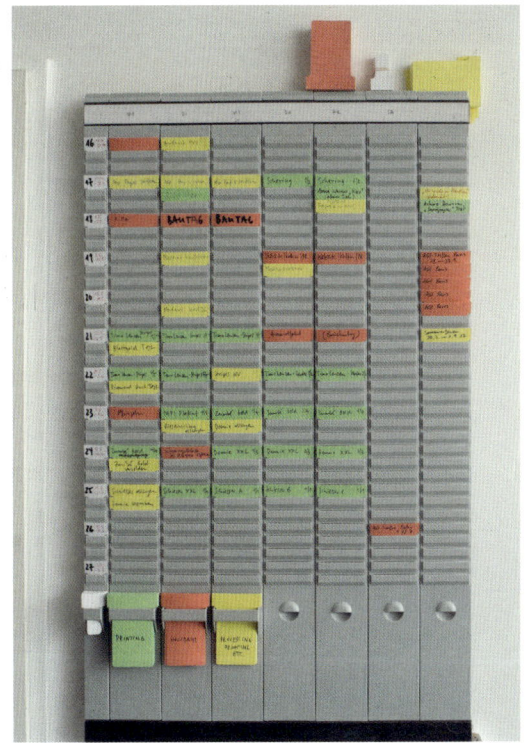

— There is no undo button.

Handsiebdruckerei is in the Berlin neighbourhood of Kreuzberg, in a building where printers have worked for over a hundred years. Spend time in the studio, and you get a sense of how they achieve such a degree of exactitude. The place is as well ordered as a circuit board, and Björn and Stefan's attention to detail comes across in everything from the armoury of squeegees to the store-bought registration tabs. Then there is their voluminous archive, drawer upon drawer of test prints and ledgers recording years of experimentation with ink and paper.

Few studios working today have been so systematic in exploring what you can do with silkscreen. Handsiebdruckerei Kreuzberg shows that, when it comes to jaw-dropping results, relentless experimentation is the key to mastery. Obsession leads to perfection.

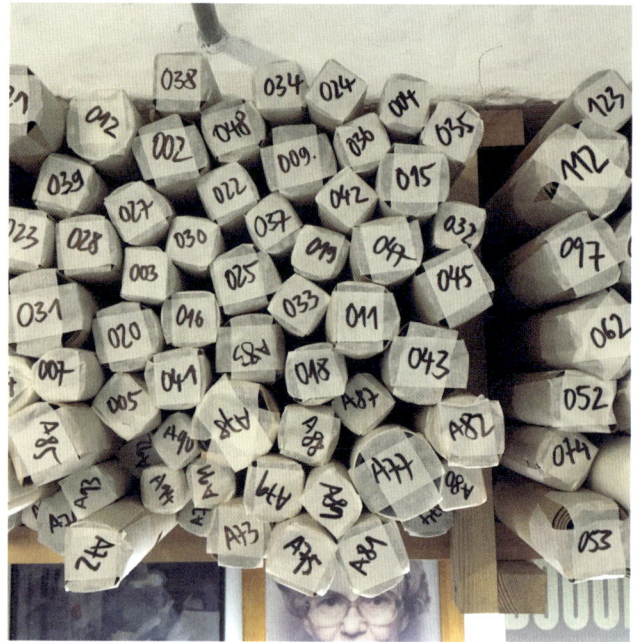

We try to reach perfection, knowing it's impossible.

Silkscreen Masters

right:
Martin Eder is a leading German painter and the founder of the experimental black metal project RUIN. Their album *HALF SKULL* was released in 2011 in a limited edition of 1000. The CD is accompanied by 12 inserts, printed in 12 different inks, variously made from a base of oil, vodka, fat, blood, soap, aspirin, tobacco, metal, bone, ash, soot, and salt. Each insert corresponds to one of its 12 tracks, and together they evoke the album's soundscape.

The research, design and printing process took several months, and was executed at Hansiebdruckerei Kreuzberg, in their incarnation as the Zwölf graphic design studio.

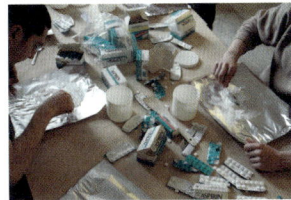

Artist Susanne Kriemann's
Duskdust project takes
as its starting point a
disused site for industrial
limestone mining on the
coast of Gotland, Sweden.
Following on from an artist's
book and collection of
monographs, this series
of 22 silkscreen prints
was made in collaboration
with Hansiebdruckerei
Kreuzberg in Berlin.

A mountain seen at dawn and
at dusk rises in the centre of
the image. In fact, it is a huge
pile of rubble, limestone that
was extracted but still hadn't
been processed when the
mining company closed. The
artist collected rocks from
the pile, and then ground
them into a dust which the
Hansiebdruckerei team
transformed into an ink, and
then printed onto rock paper.

left:
adapting large-scale
industrial processes
for textile printing at
Insley and Nash

right:
detail of fabric screen
printed at Insley and Nash

opposite page:
Les Queues de Sardines
—
Kishi stockings, 2012

Margriet Thissen

Master printer Margriet Thissen is the resident screen print expert at the Jan van Eyck Academie in the Netherlands. We asked about her experience working with large-scale formats, and about how she works with silkscreen in a more formal academic context.

below:
Margriet Thissen printing with
Joan van Barneveld in the
Charles Nypels Lab at the JVE

The Jan van Eyck Academie was founded in Maastricht, the Netherlands, in 1948, and has since become one of Europe's most dynamic art and design academies. Officially a 'post-academic institute for fine art, design and reflection', it is home to the Charles Nypels Lab, which since its revamp in 2011 has been a focal point for the world print scene (as well as venue for the Riso Biennale). Headed by Jo Frenken, it is a bright and airy second-floor space, with a plethora of printing machines and equipment.

A printer of over 30 years' experience, Margriet Thissen is the screen print expert at the Van Eyck. She explains how the studio offers print-ing services to residents, providing them with a range of possibilities, in terms of inks and substrates, and print scale. "We have a textile table where you can screen print a pattern of up to 200 cm by 520 cm. So you can think big and really use the traditional graphic techniques in a modern way for an edition, an installation, fashion, and so on."

this page:
residents who have collaborated with Margriet, clockwise from above: Jessica Segall; Cedar Lewisohn; a group meeting; Grace Schwindt's printed textile

left:
the finished screen-
printed garment by
Grace Schwindt

below:
Ebby Port's screen-
printed fashion line

Work and think in layers. Think over and over again about how the next layer should be. It is important to get each one right.

Throughout her career, Margriet has worked a lot with XXL formats, ever since she opened her own home studio in a 13th floor apartment. She has printed for fashion designers, and on costumes for performances by, among others, Alexis Blake and Grace Schwindt. She has also worked with artist Oscar Santillan on installations. "I screen print a lot of large format pieces, often on difficult materials such as transparent fabrics, very smooth Perspex, or thick cotton. This is always a challenge, but most of the time it works out very well. Even after all these years, the whole process is still very exciting – I still hold my breath before the first print comes out."

this page:
a selection from
Margriet Thissen's
spellbinding series of
landscapes, screen
printed between
2008 and 2012

To attempt photo realism in screen print is to work within a set of limitations. I was first inspired to attempt it when I had the opportunity to examine a set of prints by Richard Estes, which used carefully chosen spot colours and whole tones to build up a truer, more detailed image than one assembled from mathematical percentages of process inks. I develop my images using my own evolving set of techniques, which avoid traditional halftones and process printing in favour of layered spot colours, chosen subjectively. Anywhere from six to 20+ inks are used. Semi-transparent overlays yield additional colours as multiple inks overlap to produce a broader range of colour and texture, simulating gradation from what is essentially a series of thresholds, picked apart and reassembled in a process of trial and error.

Dan MacAdam — Crosshair

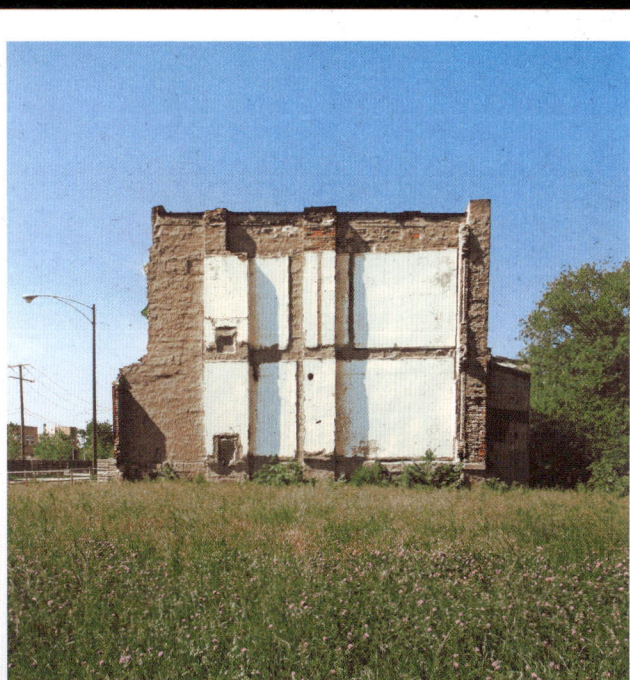

top:
Crosshair
—
Gates, 2017

above:
Crosshair
—
Gates (detail), 2017

right:
Crosshair
—
Open City, 2017

WE WERE FOCUSED ON THE FUTURE

BALANCE WOULD BE RESTORED.

left:
Strane Dizioni
—
Jesse Jacobs
Bumper Crop comic, 2017

below:
Strane Dizioni
—
Jesse Jacobs
spread from the book
Crawl Space, 2017

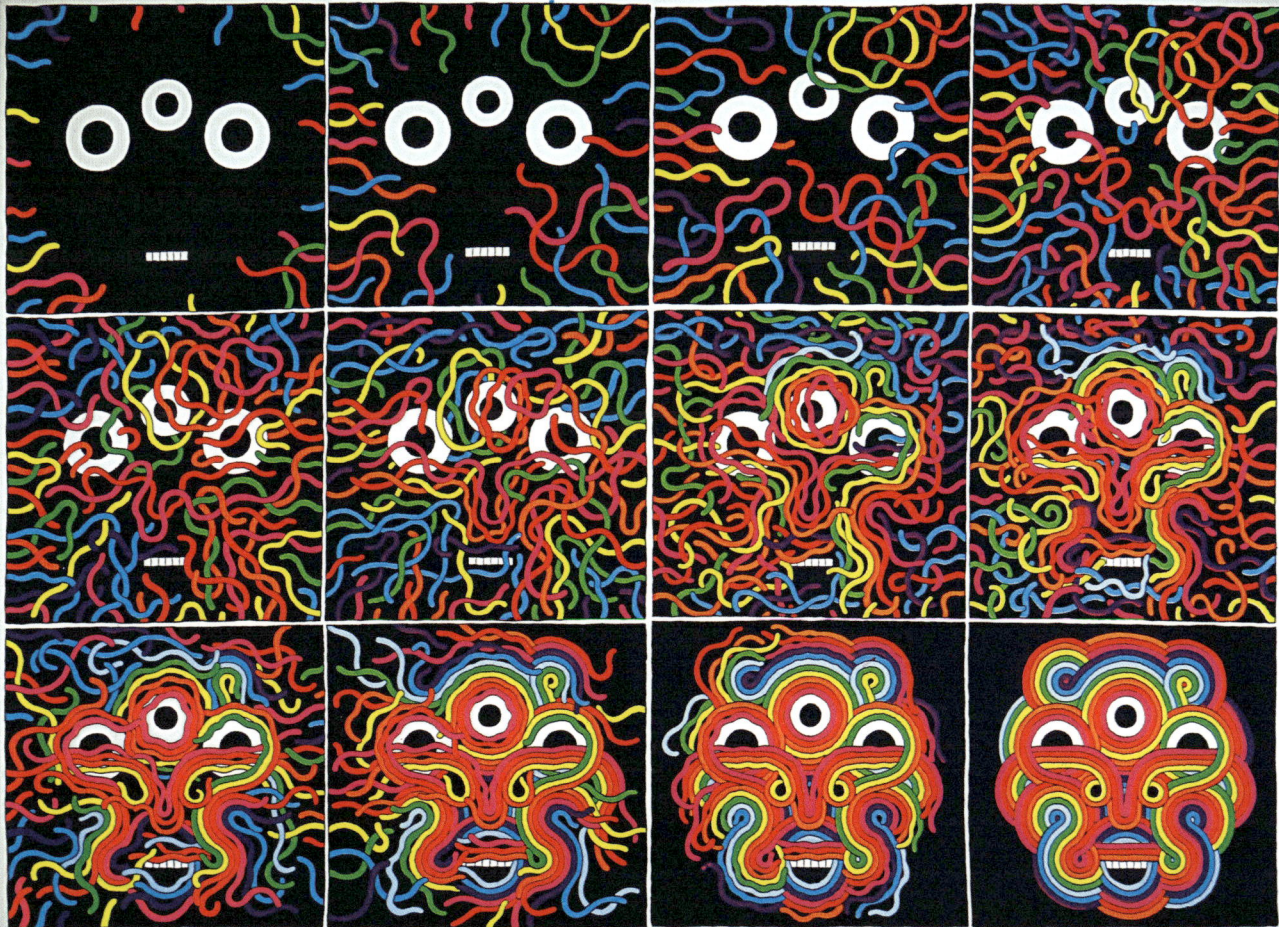

right:
Heretic/Spectral Nation
is one of the most
dynamic and experimental
screen print studios
in London today

left:
Heretic/Spectral Nation

—

Untitled, 2015

opposite page:
Heretic/Spectral Nation

—

Chromatecliptix 1 #6,
2015

Light-Sensitive Oscillators:
Learn to Make Sound Circuits

Sunday, June 16
12-4pm

Raphael Arar

Raphael Arar will teach you how to make light-sensitive oscillators for you to take home.
In the process, you'll learn a lot about basic electronics (like how to use a breadboard and how to solder) as well as sound and audio.

All materials provided

members $75
non-members $85

No electronics experience necessary

machine Project

above:
Tom Kracauer
—
Tom Kracauer and
Taylor Giali
*Light-Sensitive
Oscillators*, 2013
3-colour poster for
Machine Project,
Los Angeles

right:
Tom Kracauer
—
Tom Kracauer
and Sarah Shoemake
Ted Purves, 2013
print for the Paul Brach
Visiting Artist Lecture
Series at CalArts

Serigraffeur

Tom Singier is the owner of Serigraffeur, a Berlin gallery and store dedicated to silkscreen prints. As a printer and a designer, Tom is ideally placed to anticipate and respond to the ever-growing silkscreen market. Here, he talks about his vision and practice as a gallerist.

Serigraffeur opened in 2012, and Tom has worked there full-time for several years. He organizes regular shows, sometimes two a month. The space is a treasure trove, with rack upon rack of silkscreen posters by some of the biggest names working today. He invites artists to curate a show of their own work in the gallery space, and then sells their prints at a commission. If they don't sell, he gives them back. If they do, he buys more.

Serigraffeur only carries prints: "I don't sell t-shirts in the same way I don't sell kebabs – it's not about how well they sell." Of course, Tom says, he isn't paying the rent of any of his artists. But he is contributing something towards it, as are numerous other silkscreen galleries and spaces; all together, they keep a lot of artists in ink. Tom still thinks more like a collector than a gallerist, his approach still defined by the informality and authenticity of the DIY scene. He sees himself as having a reciprocal relationship with the community that welcomed him. By concentrating on bringing silkscreen prints to a bigger audience, he can contribute to that community, he says, and still spend all day looking at posters.

Warhol is our Godwin's law: whenever people are talking about silkscreen, sooner or later someone is going to mention Warhol. But from those pop beginnings, silkscreen has grown into a medium that is about having the widest possible freedom

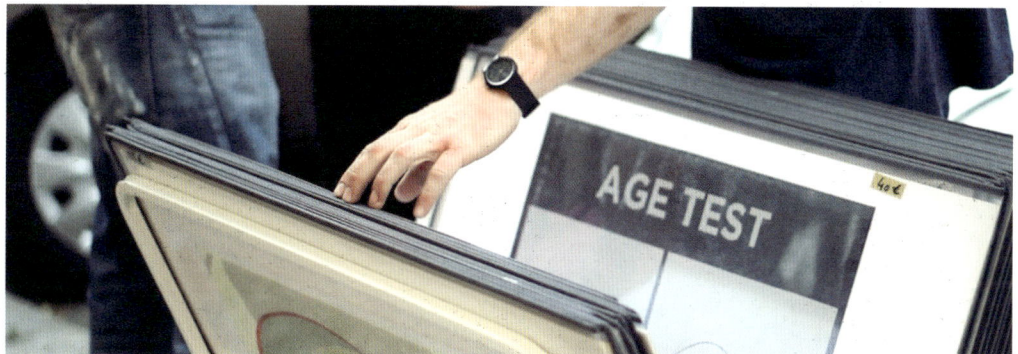

this spread:
front door always open, Serigraffeur is a bustling hub, drawing in passers-by, tourists, and print fans alike

Kid Icarus

Kid Icarus is a studio and store in Toronto's Kensington Market, run by Michael Viglione and Bianca Bickmore. One of its main philosophies is to channel historical energies and foreground the radical, democratic tradition of screen printing.

The print area at Kid Icarus is behind the counter of the store, a decision designed to provoke people's interest and draw them into the process. The studio collaborates with artists and bands, and complements its commercial print work with community-oriented projects, maintaining an active presence on the local alternative scene. "One of the things that attracted us to printmaking was the Mexican Revolution, and how the printing press was used to create propaganda through art. It was very affordable to print multiple copies, so many people had access to the images. As screen printers at a small shop, we try and follow that philosophy of making the process accessible to people who are interested in creating affordable fine art.

The challenge we all have as traditional printers is to educate the public about what we do. Digital printing has rapidly become able to print on almost anything, but we're not too concerned about it. We teach screen printing workshops twice a month, and the store helps spread the word about printing by hand. We felt that in the '90s in the US, the general public just thought of silkscreen printing as the way graphics were printed onto shirts. But nowadays we feel like the medium is becoming prevalent again, despite the rise of digital printing technology; more and more people understand the process."

above:
Kid Icarus
—
Doublenaut
poster for microbrewery
Bellwoods' 'Cat Lady' IPA

right:
Kid Icarus
—
3D Fanzine, 2017

left and opposite page:
shots of the chic and
cosy interior of the store

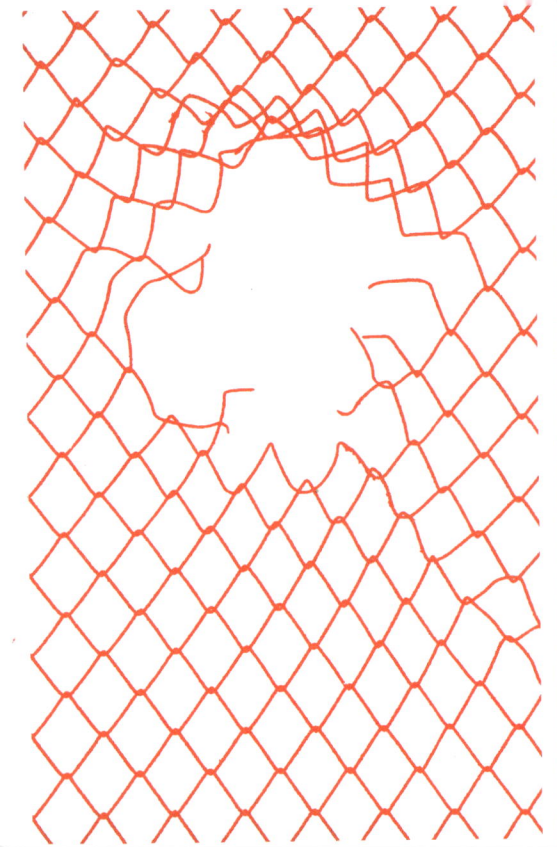

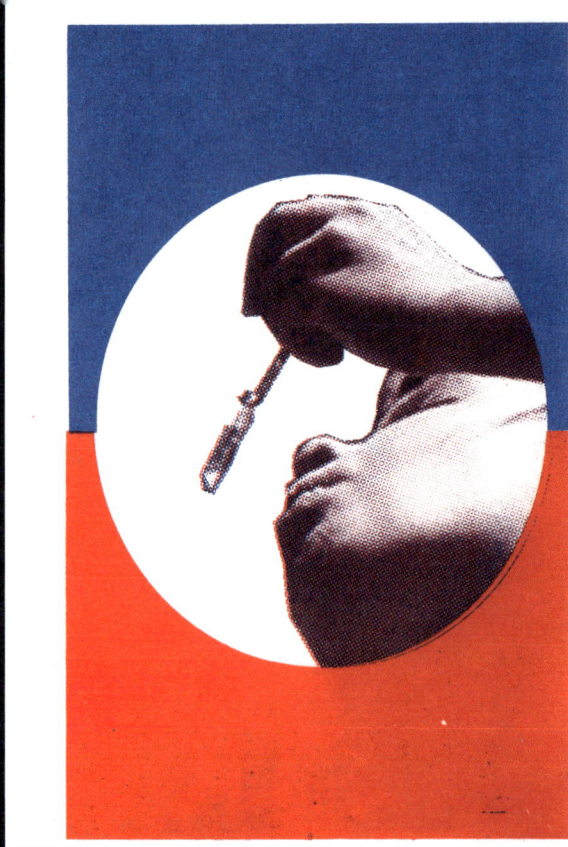

above:

Gregory Le Lay

Two prints from the
Bubble series, 2017

right:

Gregory Le Lay

Spread from the book
A Mon Bon Souvenir, 2016

left:
Taller 57

Adriana Oliver
Legs, n.d.

below left:
Taller 57
—
Miss Van
Untitled, 2016

below right:
Taller 57
—
Alldsgn for Taller 57
57, n.d.

above:
Zansky (Edições de Zaster)
—
spread from the book
Mandibula, 2017

opposite page:
Zansky (Edições de Zaster)
—
Falling Down, 2017

left and bottom left:
Zansky (Edições de Zaster)
—
Marfim Eloquente, 2015
a 24-page book in 16
colours, printed using
the direct process
method of painting
directly on the screen

below:
Zansky (Edições de Zaster)
—
Could Be Cold, 2015
experimental screen print
from a series based on
Nina Simone's version
of *Sinnerman*, photo
by Pablo de Sousa

57/90

Zansky

Silkscreen Masters - Secrets of
the World's Top Screen Printers

A Vetro Editions project

English edition published by Moleskine srl

Publishing Director
Roberto Di Puma

Author
John Z. Komurki

Art direction
Luca Bendandi

Technical consulting
Dolly Demoratti at Mother Drucker

Design
Luca Bendandi and Claudio Braina

Illustration
Leonardo González

Picture editing
Cristobal Pereira

Proofreading
Elizabeth Amato

ISBN 978-88-6613-166-3

First Edition November 2017
Printed in Italy by Galli Thierry Stampa

Cover design by Vetro Editions
featuring artwork by various artists
included and credited in the book

Vetro Editions would like to warmly thank
the many people who have been involved in
Silkscreen Masters. Among them are Céline
Remechido at Pyramyd Editions, whose interest
set the book in motion; Roberto Di Puma at
Moleskine and Mónica Gili at Editorial Gustavo
Gili, for their belief in the project; Dolly Demoratti,
whose experience and wisdom made it possible;
Hansiebdruckerei Kreuzberg, for their hospitality,
advice and patience; Leonardo González, whose
illustrations gave the manual its personality;
Claudio Braina, whose work on the layout gave
the manual its shape; Luca Bogoni, for his
suggestions on an earlier version; Elizabeth
Amato, for her infallible eagle eye; and Cristobal
Pereira, who made an invaluable contribution
as both photographer and photo editor. The
worldwide silkscreen community is welcoming,
dynamic and fun, and it's been a privilege to
interact with it. We received advice and help
from many, many people in the world of screen
printing: thank you.